POKHRAN

POKHRAN
A NOVEL

UDAY SINGH

Srishti
PUBLISHERS & DISTRIBUTORS

SRISHTI PUBLISHERS & DISTRIBUTORS
A unit of AJR Publishing LLP
212A, Peacock Lane
Shahpur Jat, New Delhi – 110 049
editorial@srishtipublishers.com

First published by
Srishti Publishers & Distributors in 2020
Copyright © Uday Singh, 2020

10 9 8 7 6 5 4 3 2 1

This is a work of fiction. The characters, places, organisations and events described in this book are either a work of the author's imagination or have been used fictitiously. Any resemblance to people, living or dead, places, events, communities or organizations is purely coincidental.

The author asserts the moral right to be identified as the author of this work.

All rights reserved. No part of this publication may be reproduced, stored in a retrieval system, or transmitted, in any form or by any means, electronic, mechanical, photocopying, recording or otherwise, without the prior written permission of the Publishers.

Dedicated to,
and in memory of my dear friend,
Niraj Dhondi.

Inspired by real events and people.

Names of people, events, locations, and dates have been modified for dramatic effect and bear no resemblance to reality. Any resemblance to real people, events, locations, and/ or dates is purely coincidental.

Contents

Acknowledgement • ix

Top Secret Smiling Buddha • xi

1. My Childhood in Pokhran • *1*

2. Hanging Out with Charvakas • *18*

3. The Friendly Dacoits • *35*

4. Deeper into the Pokhran Nuclear Blast • *56*

5. Chaitanya Gets to MIT • *70*

6. Meeting Zara • *88*

7. Marrying Zara • *104*

8. Zara Visits Syria • *122*

9. Ends Justify the Means • *140*

10. Rebuilding Pokhran • *160*

11. Chaitanya's Letter from Beyond • *177*

A note from the author • *190*

Acknowledgement

Every time I have come across a novel idea, heard of an interesting concept, or read a book, I have felt super thankful to those that came before me. Grateful that so many before me have contributed in such varied ways to make life comfortable and more interesting, at the same time propelling humanity forward. While I enjoyed all that they had to offer, I always felt it my responsibility to pay it forward and contribute to our collective human consciousness. This book is an opportunity for me to do so. I am extremely thankful to my family, friends and mentors, who have helped refine my thinking. They have guided me to develop an appreciation for novel ideas and concepts that aid humanity in our pursuit to realize our full potential.

While it has been a labour of love to get this book into its final form, it would not have been possible to do so without the diligence, hard work, and support provided by my editor, Stuti. For that, I shall forever be grateful to her. My supporter at Srishti Publishers, Arup Bose, deserves equal credit, and my gratitude for believing in me as a writer and for helping get this book published.

I would also like to extend special and heartfelt thanks to my dear friend, Sam, for being a constant source of encouragement in this endeavour. I wouldn't have made it through this far without the support of Niraj and Sam. And to Naresh, for inspiring me and for showing me courage through adversity.

Top Secret Smiling Buddha
(1970-1975)

"What took you so long, Ranvir?" Chaitanya asked calmly, with a hint of a smile, as the door swung open.

Ranvir, a tall, dishevelled and weather-beaten man in his early thirties, stood there with a revolver in his hand. As Ranvir burst into the room, trembling, with anger welling up from every pore in his body, Chaitanya leaned back in his comfortable black leather chair with the expression of a chess grandmaster who was quite content that the game had played out precisely as he had planned.

"BOOM!"

A shot rang out of the gun, piercing the soft atrophied muscles of Chaitanya. The impact toppled his body off the wheelchair and onto the white tiled floor. The blood slowly started flowing out of the gunshot wound and began to form a bright crimson cloud on the floor. Ranvir repositioned the gun to fire his second shot close to Chaitanya's heart, while Chaitanya smiled with satisfaction.

There were too many emotions and too much adrenaline coursing through Ranvir's veins to notice what was going on. He was focused on sweet revenge that would finally bring peace to his troubled mind. How long he had fantasized about this moment, about finding out who was behind all this, and how he would torture and dismember the person responsible for the pain and the anguish to Komal, his family, and his friends. Even in his wildest imaginations, he had never expected the villain to be a frail quadriplegic with such limited physical abilities, who had wreaked so much havoc. As these thoughts ran through his head, Ranvir found that his fingers and his body were beyond his own control as they squeezed hard against the trigger one more time.

"BOOM!"

Another shot rang out, and this time the bullet passed smoothly through my ribs and heart, and exited through the other side. I could feel the heat of the bullet as it passed through me and then I began to see myself rise out of that frail dead body and drift upwards.

Before you start to feel pity for me as the good guy trapped in that frail disabled body, or condemn me as the bad guy, you will have to know more. Things are never as black and white as they may seem at first glance. I could see myself floating up over my immobile body, and it was with a tinge of sadness that I looked back at the physical form that used to be me for the past forty-five years. As images of Zara, Devyani, papa and didi flashed past, I wondered whether I'd receive a similar comforting welcome that those dearly departed souls would have received in their afterlife or be relegated to something much darker which is reserved for the worst of human souls like myself.

To be certain, the seeds for my situation were sown long before I was born, when Dalai Lama fled Tibet, in the late 50s, to avoid capture by the Chinese government, and received refuge in India. For India, it was a very natural act of generosity and openness. It has provided asylum and a safe haven to many who were persecuted unfairly elsewhere – be it the Buddhist monks from Tibet, the Zoroastrians from Persia, the Khojas, the Ismailis from Persia and the Middle East, or the Egyptians. Even Cleopatra sent her seventeen-year-old son Caesarion to the Red Sea port of Berenice for safety, as part of his escape to India when Octavian invaded Egypt. Mao, the Chairman of the People's Republic of China, was irked at the support and reception Dalai Lama received, and it was Mao's bruised ego among other things that led to the Sino-Indian war in the early 60s.

Soviet Union, the supposed friend of India, was too distracted with the Cuban missile crisis to be of any help to India in her time of need during the Sino-Indian war. That was the beginning of the end of the Soviet friendship, and also an end to any notions that Nehru tried to promote about the use of nuclear power only for peaceful purposes. While the Indian nuclear program had its start right after the Sino-Indian war, the Indo-Pakistan war of 1971 provided the right impetus for the Indian nuclear program to be revitalized. Approval from the Indian Parliament led to the launch of the "Smiling Buddha" project, to build our nuclear capability for weapons use.

Maybe it was Mao's hurt ego. Maybe it was the Cuban missile crisis. Or, maybe a confluence of all those events that led India on this path and brought about the nuclear test of Pokhran, inextricably involving my life with that fateful 1974 "Smiling Buddha" nuclear test. Given such violent world events, maybe it is only fitting that my life has been violently entangled with Pokhran and refugees till the very end.

18 May 1974, Pokhran: It was a usual morning in the dry Rajasthani desert, slightly chillier than expected for that time. Not a single cloud could be seen for as far as the eye could see, and the humidity in the air was close to zero as it hadn't rained in these parts for over a decade. The turbaned men of the village had already started out of their homes with lunches tied to the end of a stick slung over their shoulders, headed to work. The women headed out on their five mile trek to fill up their pots with drinking water.

The village was used to seeing periods of hectic traffic and activity every five years, when politicians dropped by for their customary visits to their vote banks. But this traffic was very quiet and made up mostly of military trucks and jeeps which bore no similarity to that of the politicians and their hordes of cronies and political supporters with their party flags belting out party slogans and speeches over blaring loud speakers. This new and rather strange traffic was reticent, purposeful, and headed straight to the Pokhran Fort, Balagarh, that had not been in use since 1952. That was when Bhawani Singh, the last of the Champawat Rathores, handed over the ownership of the fort to the Indian government as part of the nationalization of land and property.

One day earlier, about a dozen or so trucks had arrived at the fort, carrying decorated military officers in uniform and some scientists in white coats who all milled about the place setting up things and getting ready for what seemed to be a big event. The cooks, the chambermaids and the servers had arrived a day before that to get the fort ready, in order to receive this retinue of officers and scientists. The dinner was set in the dining hall on the third and topmost floor of the fort, with a clear view of the vast Thar desert.

By 6 p.m., as the sun was on its way down, warm orange sunlight streaked through the westward facing windows of the fort. As the waiters moved about, fine dust particles rose and danced about in the sunlight. Slowly, the officers and scientists started making their way to the dining hall and began settling into their designated seats. Most of them had worked with each other over the past three years and had bonded more closely with this group than with their own families.

As the group reached a quorum, Narendra Pant, seated at the head of the dining table, stood up to address the room. He was over six feet tall, in his early fifties, clean shaven, slightly greying hair that made him look refined and distinguished. He had this constant smile, almost a grin, that exuded seniority, while at the same time made him personable and approachable. His white shirt and grey hair stood in stark contrast to the dark painting that adorned the wall behind him – capturing the Battle of Jhelum where the Macedonian king Alexander incurred significant military losses in defeating the relatively small-time Indian king, Porus.

"Thank you for clapping like you are really glad to see me. Although, I believe you all are more glad that you don't have to deal with me starting tomorrow, assuming everything goes according to plan," his eyes scanned the entire room as he spoke and paused for effect.

Gentle laughter rippled through the audience. Narendra was loved and respected. As the room became quiet again, he put out his cigarette and took a sip of his Scotch and began to speak again in his gruff slow voice.

"Let me start by saying 'Thank you' again. The best battles I have been involved in are those that I didn't have to fight. On this occasion, more than ever, the two thousand-year-old story of King Porus and Alexander is highly relevant. Brute force rarely wins wars; rather it is the right combination of bravery, cunning and propaganda that does," he said as he pushed his chair back and started walking towards the painting behind him.

Narendra spoke with his gaze locked at the painting, "Porus used bravery in his battle. Despite the small size of his army, he managed to inflict the greatest casualties that Alexander's Macedonian army had seen so far. Chanakya deployed cunning to infiltrate the ranks of Alexander's army and got Chandragupta inserted there." He was slow and deliberate as he continued to speak. It was obvious that he took great pride in the military strategy that was executed by Chanakya.

"Once inside, Chandragupta engaged in propaganda to spread rumours about the size and might of the Nanda empire's army, which was already ten times in size to that of Porus' army. It was ultimately the rumours that made Alexander back away from attacking India (the then Nanda empire) any further, as there was a mutiny within the Macedonian army. Alexander's army officers rebelled against going on such a suicide mission." He paused and surveyed the room.

"That is an excellent example of effective deterrence, when wars are not fought at all, when you scare the living daylights out of your enemy just by your existence," his voice rose in pitch as his face lit up with enthusiasm.

There was utter silence and even the waiters stopped to listen to his speech. He slowly walked to the edge of the table and looked across the room, "We are gathered here today, on this historic occasion, to create a similar deterrence against the threats we face today. So that we may not have to fight anymore battles."

"To Indian deterrence!" He raised his glass to make a toast, and the whole room erupted with applause. Everyone stood up to join in the toast.

Narendra was a master of timing, had perfect diction, and most importantly, he knew people. He had the rare ability to readily connect with people at all levels, from the waiter to the commander, and when he was talking to you, he would hold your gaze and make you feel that what you have to say is the most important thing for him. On top of that, he had a fantastic memory. As the applause quieted down, he glanced around the room and waited for people to settle down again.

"Please convey a debt of gratitude from the entire country and myself to your families for putting up with the long hours, moving to Trombay to work on this project and for keeping it a secret from your family and friends."

He pointed to Suresh, one of the quantum physicists on the project, who was seated ten seats away on the right. "Suresh, you've been in the doghouse with your wife because she thinks you are having an affair. Tomorrow, you will finally be able to tell the truth and get your wife and also your life back." He smiled while the entire audience burst out laughing.

Suresh smiled and shot back at Narendra, "I will demolish you on the hockey field tomorrow, for that!"

"Please take your seats. Enough of me taking up this air time. I would like to invite Subramaniyam Iyengar, the real brain behind this project, to say a few words." Narendra sat down and returned to his Scotch as the room erupted in whistles and applause once more.

The fluorescent lights came on inside the dining hall, as it had become dark outside. The warm desert breeze became chilly as the temperature dipped along with the sun. The open areas of the fort were still dark and lighting was kept to a bare minimum so as to not attract any attention, with the overhead US and Soviet surveillance satellites. Although everybody around the table was tense in anticipation of tomorrow's event, they were slowly beginning to enjoy themselves. As the waiters replaced the plates and refilled the glasses across the table, Subramaniyam got up to speak.

In his white lab coat and heavy black-rimmed glasses, Subramaniyam looked like he would be more comfortable and a better fit in his surroundings if he were in a university cafeteria debating scientific theories with other faculty members rather than rubbing shoulders with macho military heads. This was the opportunity of a lifetime for him to push his own limits and to take India to the next level, joining the ranks of the other five nuclear nations. He had lucrative job offers waiting for him in the US – right after he completed his Ph.D. from MIT in Cambridge in his twenty-fourth year – when he was recruited into this program.

"I owe a debt of gratitude to Narendra for recruiting me right out of college into this program and for believing in me enough to work on my dream project," Subramaniyam spoke in a low tone, as if unsure of himself.

"This has been a complex undertaking involving multiple disciplines, including metallurgy, chemical explosives, quantum physics, radioactivity and manufacturing weaponry, among other things. Huge thanks go to Suresh Rao, Rajesh Garg, Ankit Ratnakar and others from the Bhabha Atomic Research Centre who have been an integral part of bringing this program to this point." He looked at each one of them around the table as he expressed thanks.

His voice took on a more confident tone and his posture changed as he began speaking again. "A lot could go wrong tomorrow!" he paused. "Although we have tested and retested our processes and systems, a lot can go wrong as this is an implosion-bomb and its mechanism is not simple. About twenty chemical bombs have to explode at the same time for the nuclear bomb to go off." He was in his element now, these were his students and he was their professor.

"Imagine, where I am standing right now, to be the core or the centre of the bomb, where all the fissile plutonium is placed. And now imagine twenty train tracks, each coming in from a different direction, leading to me at the centre."

For the first time since he started speaking, the room became totally quiet, as if everyone present was holding their breath. "Now imagine for a moment that the twenty locomotive engines, one on each of those twenty tracks barrelling down at tremendous speed, have to meet at this very point where I am standing, all of them at precisely the same time."

Given his risk-averse nature, he had to throw in a word of caution. "If the timing or the speed or the weight of one of the engines is off, it would throw the whole thing in disarray and we will have to start all over again. All this preparation would go waste and it could potentially take us a year or more to get back together again." At these sobering words, the whole room fell silent as if the positive energy and spirit of merriment was sucked away from the audience, replaced by a dread of failure.

At that point, Narendra got up. "That is a fantastic explanation, Subramaniyam. And that is why we have you and the best brains in India working on this. You know, my wife tells me that I sound smarter on days that I have interacted with you," he quipped, lightening the mood as the audience began chuckling and laughing again.

"Before we close for the night, are there any questions or comments from anyone?" Narendra asked, looking across the room.

Rajni Hegde, editor of The Times of India magazine, asked the most humane and what seemed like an anti-patriotic question in that setting overflowing with national pride and patriotism. "Have you considered the impact to the surrounding human life as a result of the nuclear fallout, in the event of a successful detonation?"

That question took a lot of courage for her to ask, as the reaction from almost everyone in that room was more of disdain, as if the cost if any would be way worth the price of having a successful nuclear weapon. All the looks were focused on her and despite those gazes, Rajni stayed firm and looked around the room for an answer.

Finally, Subramaniyam got up, and said, "We built explosion models anticipating around twenty kiloton yield, and based on that our recommendation is to conduct the test in an underground bunker that is a hundred feet deep. This will ensure that there will be no nuclear fallout and hence no negative impact to the human or animal life in the surrounding areas."

Having reviewed images and stories of pain and suffering from the Hiroshima and Nagasaki nuclear aftermaths, Rajni wasn't convinced of the accuracy of the models, but she decided not to press on. She was smart enough to recognize that, for her humanitarian questions, the train had already left the station.

"If there are no further questions, wrap up your dinner and drinks as soon as possible as we have a big day tomorrow. The "Smiling Buddha" nuclear bomb is being transported to the test bunker as we speak. We will be meeting in the basement of this fort, which will serve as the Command Centre for conducting all our operations, at 4 a.m. sharp."

"Good night and Jai Hind!" Narendra gulped down the remainder of the Scotch in his glass, stubbed out his cigarette and retired to his room.

Subramaniyam could not go back to his room right away, as the last question from Rajni brought back concerns about the accuracy of the nuclear explosion models.

Suresh used to mock at those models as they didn't take into account a whole lot of variables. As he retired to his room and laid on his bed, he kept tossing and turning as if he was a death row inmate to be executed tomorrow. And he could not shake off the terrible feeling that something was not right.

While the pensive military officers and scientists tried to sleep in the fort, a few kilometres away, there was frenetic activity starting with Balbir Bakhshi, a short portly man in his late forties, very affable and loved by his brigade, shouting orders to his jawans, directing them on the delicate handling of the precious cargo being transported to Ground Zero.

"Start clearing the tracks!" Balbir shouted on his speaker, as the soldiers started firing up the handheld petromax lamps lighting the railway tracks so that the workers could clear out the sand that kept the tracks hidden from prying eyes or overhead satellites.

The cargo was placed on an uncovered rail car, guarded by a company of over twenty soldiers armed with machine guns. Those soldiers were personally hand-picked for this task by both Narendra and Balbir. The guards were informed that it was top secret, but they were not told what the contents of the cargo were when it was loaded up on the train that left its origination point at Trombay. Having arrived at Chandan station via Jaisalmer over the public railway tracks, the nuclear cargo was about ten kilometres from Ground Zero. This last leg of its journey had to be completed on the secret tracks laid down specifically for this day. The workers had no more than two hours to clear the tracks from Chandan to Ground Zero, and get them ready for the cargo to be delivered to its final destination.

"Lights out!" an order from Balbir was relayed across the tracks less than one hour after they had started working on them. Balbir had his clear orders and the intel on the timings of the US surveillance satellites, to ensure that the activities in and around Ground Zero stay off the international radar till after the test the next day.

Some of the soldiers lit cigarettes and others just plopped themselves by the tracks in silence, waiting for surveillance clearance to start digging again.

"Lights on and start clearing tracks!" The order came over the speakers after fifteen minutes had elapsed.
Right about midnight, when the tracks were cleared, Balbir placed a call to Narendra, "Sir, Smiling Buddha is ready to leave Chandan for Ground Zero. Do I have your clearance?"

"Yes. You have my OK, Balbir," Narendra replied.

"Guards, get on the train!" Balbir shouted into the speakers.

"Sumeet, you have clearance to start and keep the pace at a steady ten kmph and avoid any sudden movements in order not to disturb the cargo," Balbir walked up to the engine master. The excitement and anticipation was too much for Balbir to notice the nice warmth provided by the engine furnace against the chilly desert night. He patted Sumeet on his back and jumped off the engine to join the guards stationed in the rail cars behind the cargo.

With a steamy hiss and a loud clang, as the brake separated from the engine wheels, the massive black steam engine started rolling towards Pokhran. It was an uneventful one hour train ride, but it felt like an eternity to Balbir and the guards.

The train came to a halt at the gate guarding Ground Zero, waiting for Balbir to share the authorization papers with the guards at the gate, before the gate was opened again, allowing the train to reach the centre, where a heavy duty crane was waiting to lower the cargo into "Smiling Buddha" cellar that was dug a hundred feet below the ground.

As the hands of the fort clock landed on 3 a.m., Balbir looked at his watch with satisfaction, knowing that they were doing better than expected with regards to time.

"Anish, the "Smiling Buddha" is all yours," Balbir handed over the authorization papers to Anish Saxena, a tall lanky man in his fifties with sunken eyes and an elongated face. A mask was covering his nose and mouth, and gloves over his hands made him look like a surgeon about to go into the operating theatre. He was the commanding officer for hooking up the detonation coils, sensors and performing countdown checks prior to the detonation of the device.

Anish and his team of electrical engineers had practised this task with a blank prototype in preparation for this day. They were ready, or at least as ready as they could possibly be. There was a ton of TNT loaded in the bomb and there was no room for error.

"Take off the tarpaulin," Anish ordered, revealing the bomb as Balbir looked on. This was the first time Balbir got to lay his eyes on the "Smiling Buddha", as it was hoisted on a concrete block with a curved surface to accommodate the spherical shape of the bomb that was about four feet across and weighed about one-and-a-half tons. Balbir's chest swelled with pride at being a part of this historic moment for India.

"We have exactly one hour to hook up the twenty detonators to the detonation coil and start the yield gauges and the sensors. Go!" Anish blasted the order and his team got busy connecting the bomb to the central distribution coil that was connected to the switch in the basement of Fort Balagarh.

Their practice and expertise was on full display as the team moved about effortlessly, completing about a thousand electrical connections in less than one hour, and by the time the clock struck 4 a.m., they all had stopped working. The bomb was all connected and ready to be powered up.

Anish and Balbir thanked their teams for a job well done and got into the military jeep that was waiting to take them to the basement in the Pokhran fort.

Back at the fort, the officers and scientists started trickling into the Command Centre, a windowless large room in the basement with pink granite walls, makeshift chairs and tables arranged like in a classroom, and getting themselves comfortable in their designated stations monitoring the various aspects of detonating the bomb and collecting data from the gauges and the sensors before and after the blast. The waiters were around to serve coffee, tea and snacks for anyone who was up so early in the morning.

At the head of the makeshift Command Centre were ten television sets, with nine of them showing the footage of Ground Zero from different angles on the surface and one showing the bomb itself as it sat beautifully nestled in its concrete bed.

Narendra, in a crisp white shirt and perfectly parted grey hair, looked well rested, even though he had hardly slept, coordinating the delivery and installation of the bomb in its place throughout the night.

In stark contrast, Subramaniyam – with his groggy eyes and dishevelled hair – looked even more like an absent-minded professor than he did on the previous night at the dinner. His mind was restlessly running through the various aspects of the bomb design and detonation sequences, and the potential consequences if the test failed. And more importantly, the consequences if it succeeded!

Despite the wee hours of the morning, the excitement and the energy in the room was palpable. As the clock struck 4:00, Narendra asked, "Are we ready to begin running the tests?" looking at Subramaniyam.

Subramaniyam nodded in agreement, and signalled his team to start the tests.

"Structural integrity, OK," reported the mechanical engineering team.

"Seismographs in all the locations, OK," came the geology team.

"Detonation coil 1, OK." And so on, the reports started coming in from the different teams monitoring different aspects of the "Smiling Buddha".

By 8:00, the warm sun was already up, and villagers were going about their morning chores oblivious of the very thing that was to change their lives forever. The tests were complete and all the systems were ready to go.

Suddenly, the silence and the anticipation in the Command Centre was interrupted by the loud ringing of the telephone that was at the centre of the room. Narendra got up from his seat and walked up to the telephone as if he was waiting for this call.

"Ms Prime Minister, we are all set to go. Do we have your confirmation?" he asked of the caller.

"Yes, you have my confirmation. Good luck and make us proud. Jai Hind!" The sure voice of Mrs Gandhi, the then Indian Prime Minister, came over the speakers filling the entire room.

The whole room erupted in applause and shouts of "Jai Hind!" in concert with her.

"Begin the countdown!" echoed Narendra as he hung up the phone.

Once the countdown was complete, Narendra walked up and positioned himself near the red detonation button. Despite his years of military training and forceful personality, one could see his hand tremble as it reached down and pushed the button at precisely 8:05 a.m.

There was a sudden gasp and then total silence in the room. Nobody moved as the anticipation was unbearable. And then,

"BOOM!"

The shock wave from the blast hit them. The intensity of it caught everybody by surprise, shaking the entire fort to its very foundations and knocking the dishes, chandeliers and chairs down from their places. With a yield of about twelve kilotons, the shock wave from the "Smiling Buddha" was the equivalent of a seven magnitude earthquake on the Richter scale.

Slowly, as the realization set in, the room broke out into a party with everybody hugging each other, throwing up their military hats, and patting each other on their backs for what they had managed to pull off that day.

As the din of the celebration died down, Narendra took to the stage one last time.

"This will go down in history as a major turning point in the life of our young country. Columbus, Vasco De Gama, Herodotus and other Europeans kept searching for shorter routes to get to India because we were a hardworking, intelligent and organized people who produced some of the best man-made products available on the planet at that time. Today, you have demonstrated that with seventy-five of our people, just a handful from this vast and peaceful country, we could build and detonate a nuclear bomb in Pokhran that took thousands of people for US to build in Los Alamos."

There was a gentle applause as Narendra continued, "Today, we have broadcast to the world, without uttering a single word, that we can keep a secret. We managed to evade sophisticated surveillance both by US and Soviet satellites to execute this detonation in absolute stealth mode. No one could track our developments over the past couple of years, or the transfer of the machinery from Trombay, or get anyone of us to spill the secret beyond this core team."

"Today, we have showcased our capacity to plan to the last minute detail and execute with such phenomenal precision and impact. Today, we have broken out of the past colonial stereotypes. Today, we have arrived onto the world stage. Today, we can say Jai Hind and be really proud of our country and our people!"

As he got off the stage, everybody stood up and kept the applause going for several minutes. There were tears of joy, of pride, of a job well done and of optimism for the future of India. They all knew that together they had accomplished something that neither of them would have been able to do alone.

While everyone else in the basement was caught up in the euphoria of the moment, Subramaniyam and Rajni never took their eyes off the television sets showing the footage of the Ground Zero. Approximately ten seconds after the detonation, one of the cameras captured a small puff of dust, like a small cloud that pushed out of the crater and got blown away by the wind before anyone could notice it. Just as the puff of dust rose up and vanished from the screen, the two exchanged glances with extreme fear filled in them.

Outside and away from the fort, life was pretty much the same as it was yesterday or the day before, except for the earthquake tremors. The tremors scared the birds, confused and rattled the camels, the nilgai, and the deer that roamed freely in those regions. Those working in the salt fields had to rush back to their carts to hold down and comfort their camels to prevent a stampede. Once the tremors passed, life in Pokhran returned to normal. Or so it seemed.

Paramvir Kumar was an architect and structural engineer charged with building the freshwater canal that would bring drinking water to Pokhran and other villages. He walked the whole length of the canal, looking for cracks or leaks. Although he had designed the canal to withstand high magnitude earthquakes, he had not had the opportunity to test that out until today. Once his tour and visual inspection of the canal was complete, he stood back with a smile and a sense of pride.

"India joins the exclusive nuclear club," one paper proclaimed.

"France congratulates India on her successful nuclear test," another paper affirmed.

"Pakistan does not consider the nuclear test a peaceful one," read another.

"India arrives on the nuclear world stage in absolute secrecy," headlined a US newspaper.

As was his daily routine, at exactly 6 a.m. the following day, Paramvir sat in his chair with that day's paper in one hand and a steaming hot tea-cup in another, while his wife Rajashree was busy cooking breakfast.

"Did you know that the tremor we felt yesterday morning was actually a nuclear test, about twenty kilometres from here?" he shouted out to his wife with clear excitement in his voice.

"That was scary, Papa," the nine-year-old Radhika chirped innocently while helping her mother in the kitchen.

"I hope they don't do any more of that. The whole house rattled," Rajashree replied from the kitchen.

Paramvir shook his head, as if annoyed at her lacklustre response, "You don't understand. This is such a historic moment for India. It is something we all should be proud of. And you know that, my canal design was able to handle those tremors," he added with clear excitement and pride in his voice. "They say the blast was the equivalent of a magnitude seven earthquake. My design and our construction of the canal managed to survive it without any breaks or leaks. This is the first time my interlocking tile design has been put to such a test and my builders checked and verified that it passed with flying colours!"

"I know that you are the best engineer around. I never doubted that your design would not work." Rajashree looked at her husband adoringly, set the plates of delicious looking poha on the table and stopped long enough to bend down and give him a hug.

Chapter 1
My Childhood in Pokhran
(1975-1985)

After almost a decade-long drought, it had started raining heavily since afternoon on that fateful day in late January of 1975. As the sun set and the day started to fade into the twilight, Rajashree suddenly felt her water break and started going into labour. Paramvir, who was seated in his usual chair in the verandah going over his work while sipping his evening tea, rushed into the kitchen at Radhika's cries.

Paramvir had planned for this moment, but had not anticipated such heavy and uncharacteristic rain in Pokhran. The rains had caused flooding across all the low-lying roads in and around the area, cutting off any motorized traffic. As a result of the flooding, there were no buses or taxis available that night to transport Rajashree to Jaisalmer, the closest town with any decent hospital or nursing home. The only other way to get her there was a camel cart, but that would take longer than she had time for.

So, despite his grave concerns, he was left with no options but to call the village midwife over. Even before the midwife arrived, a couple of the neighbouring women, friends of Rajashree, came over to provide comfort to her as she went into labour. One of them started stocking the room with clean sheets of cloth while the other one went into the kitchen to get the water heated and ready before the midwife arrived. Radhika sat next to her mother, arranging the pillow and holding her mother's palms in her tiny hands, excited at the thought of a baby brother while at the same time terrified at the agony and pain that her mother was experiencing. She had never seen her mother that vulnerable before. Paramvir pensively paced in and out of the room, not sure of how or what he could help with as he impatiently waited for the midwife to arrive.

"Saab, aap baahar baithiye," the midwife asked Paramvir to leave the room and sit outside as she expertly took control of the situation.

"Beta, aap jaa kar kuchh saaf kapda lekar aaiye," she directed the ten-year-old Radhika to bring along some clean clothes.

Paramvir stepped out into the verandah and walked into the cool night desert air that was mixed with the drizzle from the rain. For the first time in his life he found himself hoping and wishing that there was someone up there watching over and making things go smoothly that night. He loved his Rajashree very much, as she was the only one who truly understood him.

Paramvir was one of the early civil engineering graduates in 1960s, and had a lot of options to find work across the country as quite a few dams and canals were being commissioned and built as part of the central five-year plan. But he chose to come to Pokhran, because that is where Rajashree was from.

In many ways, they were complete opposites of each other. Rajashree was born in Pokhran, the only daughter of the headmaster of the Pohkran school. Being the only child, she was pampered and wilful, but she was also very thoughtful about helping her family and her village. Paramvir, on the other hand, was born in a small lush green village of Payradanga, in West Bengal. His father was an uneducated mason who built houses. He was the eldest of four siblings, reserved, and almost incapable of expressing softer emotions.

At a time when girls didn't go to school, Rajashree fought with her father and others to get educated till tenth standard and then subsequently to work as a teacher in the same school. She was way ahead of her times in terms of women's rights as she firmly believed in women doing more than just housework, and she made sure that at a personal level she had the freedom to pursue her passions and interests, no matter how bad the opposition from her family and the surrounding people was.

As a kid, Paramvir was always interested in building things and when he cleared his tenth standard, his teachers made sure that he applied to Calcutta Engineering College where he was admitted right away. He was fiercely patriotic and cared about building the newly independent India by becoming one of the best civil engineers that were coming out of that college.

It was about five years back, when Paramvir was visiting Pokhran as part of his college field work, to conduct the feasibility study on the canal, that he first saw Rajashree. He was invited for lunch at the headmaster's house, as he was the only educated person in the village. The headmaster and the villagers wanted to make the best impression on the engineer who had the power to authorize and commission the canal work that would bring much needed water to their village. Paramvir was fully prepared to deal with the headmaster and the villagers, but he was least expecting to be blown away by a desert maiden.

"*Beta, thanda paani le aao humare engineer saab ke liye,*" the headmaster called out in the direction of the kitchen, as Paramvir stepped into the headmaster's house on that hot sunny day.

When Rajashree came out in a yellow Rajasthani *lehenga* with a translucent red *pallu* draped over her head, a nose ring and bangles that made a tinkling sound as she poured water into his glass, Paramvir was mesmerized. He had come there to assess the canal, but did not expect to fall head over heels for this girl in such a remote village.

The moment he got back to Payradanga, he got his parents to visit Pokhran and they were married within that year. Rajashree continued to work as a teacher and made sure that her freedom and rights were respected. He admired that quality in her, the desire and willingness to fight for equality and persistence to get what she wanted. She made him complete, he couldn't ask for anything more.

During their first year of marriage, Rajashree came home one day and announced that she wanted to adopt Radhika, a six-year-old student from her school. Radhika was orphaned when her mother died of a heatstroke, while fetching water from a faraway well. Her father had left them both a long time back. As with all their other decisions, Rajashree would make a suggestion or a recommendation and Paramvir always went along, accepting her suggestion. And soon after that, Radhika was part of their happy family.

Last summer, when Paramvir and Rajashree found out that she was pregnant, it was the happiest time of their lives. Radhika was ecstatic to have a baby to play with.

Rajashree wanted the baby to be named "Chaitanya" if it was a boy, or "Roshnee" if it was a girl. She wanted the baby to bring awakening and intelligence to her village. It was important for her that the people in her village got to live better and happier lives, and she wanted her baby to help towards that goal.

"The baby is coming. Get the for water here, now!" shouted the midwife from inside the house, and that sudden shout jolted him back to reality. He was back in the present, waiting anxiously to hear the baby cry or some kind of invite for him to get back into the room and see Rajashree and the baby. And after what seemed like an eternity, there was the unmistakable cry of a baby.

Paramvir felt every cell in his body come to life as he rushed into the house. And that is where his excitement stopped. The baby, still covered in blood from the womb with the umbilical cord still intact, was born without limbs. In place of his arms and legs, there were short stubs of flesh but no palms or fingers and no feet or toes. He did not know how to react to that; he just froze without any expression, as he didn't want to rattle Rajashree who was in too much of pain to notice anything just yet.

The baby kept crying incessantly.

None of that seemed to bother the midwife. She went about her work without any hesitation. She knew that she had to clean and wipe the baby and wrap him snugly in a fresh soft cloth and hand him to the mother for the baby to keep quiet, as she had done with so many other babies in the village. There was no time for anybody else to react, as she ordered everybody around to do their jobs as she prepared the baby.

Once she wrapped and packed the baby, she handed him over into the eagerly awaiting arms of the new mother. The moment Rajashree took him in her arms, he went quiet. Tears rolled down Paramvir's hardened cheeks as he saw the immense joy and happiness in his wife's face.

Even though she continued to be in pain, she mustered enough strength to speak out and call him "Chaitanya" and hugged him and kissed his forehead. Right next to her at her bedside was Radhika, who could not stop jumping with joy!

"*Aur saaf kapda chaahiye,*" the midwife shouted out orders with concern in her voice, asking for more clean clothes.

"*Yeh lahoo nahin ruk raha,*" she continued, as the bleeding did not stop as it should have by now.

Something went terribly wrong during the childbirth, and despite all the midwife's efforts, the bleeding could not be stopped. In the early hours of the morning, Rajashree succumbed to her blood loss, holding Chaitanya in her arms.

It was left to Paramvir and Radhika to take care of Chaitanya. Paramvir was devastated and threw himself headlong into his work, so it was the ten-year-old Radhika who took care of Chaitanya when he was a baby.

"You were a naughty kid!" Radhika didi would tell me, whenever she would talk about my childhood. "The moment you started crawling, you were unstoppable, crawling to all the corners in the house and getting under the sofa, pulling the almirah, pushing the table or the chair. I had to constantly keep a look out so that you didn't hurt yourself," she would lovingly tap me on my head as she reminisced about the past.

Our papa was as strict as any father could ever be. I don't recall a single time he hugged me or spoke to me lovingly. I always wondered whether he blamed me for mom's death. Maybe if I wasn't born, then she would still be around. Growing up, there were more times I remember hating him more than thinking kindly of him.

"Don't pick him up. He has to get back into bed himself," that was his order to didi, as she tried to pick me up and carry me to bed when I was about five years old.

"Why not? He seems very tired and he doesn't seem to have the energy," Didi replied gingerly, not wanting to spoil papa's mood.

"Because I say so," would be his final response and there was no scope for further discussion.

Didi would give me a bath in the morning and dress me. In the night, she would help me into my chadar and tuck me in for the night. The rest of the day, I did things by myself as papa wanted me to, otherwise he would get angry and furious.
To be fair, he was also nice to me once in a while.

I was about six years old, when papa came home with a big long cardboard box that had arrived in the post delivered to his office. I could see his excitement as he opened the box. In the box were two prosthetic arms with flexible leather-lined sockets that would wrap around my stubs. Didi was looking on excitedly as well, as he put those arms on me and tightened the belts to hold them in place.

"Move the right hand," he said, "and now, move the left."

It was better than any gift that I had received so far. They had a pincer at the front end that allowed me to grab onto a pencil or a spoon, and a joint at the elbow that allowed the arm to be bent at an angle. By the evening, I had learnt to operate the pincers on both the ends by using the other arm and also to bend the elbow using the support of the wall or table and to straighten it out using my other arm.

"Starting today, both of you will be sitting on the chairs at the dinner table," he announced looking at both of us, as it was approaching dinner time. Prior to that day, didi and I always ate our dinner sitting on the floor as she would feed me, while papa sat at the table. We were expected to be on time at the dinner table if we wanted to get dinner that night.

That night, didi had a spring in her step as she went about setting food at the dinner table. She was excited about the new developments, about the prosthetic arms and the hint of happiness in Papa's face. The entire house was filled with subdued optimism and joy. Once the plates and glasses were set up, she reached out to lift me up and seat me in one of the dining chairs.

"No. He will be getting on the chair himself," Papa declared.

There began my arduous task of hauling myself onto the chair. It took me over fifteen minutes, but it felt like forever, as I struggled to get on the chair and seat myself, while didi held the chair tightly to prevent it from tipping over. Finally when I got on it, despite my bruised limbs, I felt like I had achieved something phenomenal. I was on top of the world.

"Clap! Clap!" Didi applauded and kissed me on my cheek with admiration.

"Put on his arms and hand him the spoon," he said sternly, looking at didi.

"Didi, you don't have to feed me anymore!" I shouted with joy, as I took my first bite with the spoon attached to my arm. I tried to maintain a brave front and carry on as normally as I could while papa was around. I was scared of him, but I also wanted him to like me. I wanted him to be proud of me.

Despite his bad temper and loveless affection, we both loved papa dearly. I knew that my newfound freedom and independence offered by my prosthetic arms would not have been possible had papa not taken me to the doctor in Jaipur couple of months earlier. The purpose of the visit was to find out what if anything was wrong with me, given my condition and whether there was anything doctors could do to make me whole again.

"Although we have no real explanation for why he was born that way, the closest reasoning I can offer is that the disabilities might have been caused by radioactive fallout from the nuclear test that was done near Pokhran right around the time your wife was pregnant with him," the doctor theorized.

"Why do you believe that to be the case, doctor?" asked papa.

This was a big shock for him, that the same thing that he was proud of could be the cause for so much pain and suffering for his family.

"I have seen a few other cases of children with disabilities from that area, who were also born around the same time as Chaitanya, and who also have no prior family history of disabilities in their ancestry. But as there is no talk about the radioactive fallout anywhere in the media or medical studies surrounding it, I can't be certain," he elaborated.

"If that is true, our government should be doing more to help out such children and the families affected by the radioactive fallout. And our media should also be reporting this so that the citizens are better informed," Papa replied, with clear disappointment in his voice that the government and the media were not doing their jobs properly.

"Although I can't help with what has happened in the past, we can certainly help him have a better quality of life going forward," the doctor proclaimed with positive energy in his voice.

After that visit to the doctor, we hadn't spoken on the subject any further, until papa walked in with that box of prosthetic arms. They changed my life completely. But more importantly, I understood, maybe for the first time, that he did care for me.

Rare were the times when we had seen or felt papa being truly happy. The nagging feeling in the back of my head would always persist that it was probably me, being the way that I was born, that left him angry and frustrated. No matter how hard I tried to behave and be good, it just never was enough.

There was this one time, when I was about eight years old, and I was coming in from outside, where I would usually sit under the khejri tree to read as I liked being surrounded by the chatter and the activities of the other village kids to keep me company. The *khejri* tree was at the end of our street and had a raised circular platform around it that served as a good congregating place for adults in the afternoon to rest under its shade and for kids in the evening to gather and play.

On that particular day, Someshwar who everyone called Somu, showed up right as I was making my way home. He was the street bully, picking on almost everyone, especially me because I was a slow and easy target. Although he would call me names and tease me, I never gave him the satisfaction of seeing the hurt that he caused me, as I would always be smiling and act as if insults were just rolling off of me.

On that day, as I was returning home to dinner, he kept blocking my path towards home. No other kids in that street dared go against him. I scanned the street to look for didi, who managed to stand up against Somu, but she was nowhere in sight. It was getting dark and I knew I had to be at the dinner table on time, and Somu was persistent in keeping the street blocked.

I had no choice but to take the long path home that went around the houses and through the hot desert sand, delaying my return home. By the time I got to my dining chair, it was well past our standard dinner time of 7 p.m.

"You realize that you are late?" Papa asked me in a cold steely voice.

"Yes. But...," I meekly protested, and before I could complete—

"Get down from that chair! No dinner for you, and no buts!" he ordered. "Get into that closet," he thundered. That was his punishment for us. He believed that we all inherently know what the right behaviour or action is, and that it will come to us if we just focus and reflect on it long enough. Locking us in the closet was his way of making us reflect and also burnish it in our minds not to repeat that mistake again.

Didi stopped eating and looked on helplessly and I knew there was no point providing any explanation. I quietly got away from the chair and dragged myself into that closet.

"Think about what you have done, and once you have reflected on this behaviour of yours, I will let you out," he spoke as he turned on the light switch and closed the closet door. The punishment closet was a windowless room the size of a car with some books, bags of grains and an incandescent light hanging from the ceiling. I was never sure what to reflect on, and I would just sit there and wait for the door to open.

About an hour later, he dropped by and asked, "Have you thought about what you have done?"

"Yes," I responded, not wanting to be locked in that closet any longer.

"What did you think about?" he enquired.

"Not to ever be late, no matter what," I replied, knowing that was the only answer that would satisfy him.

"Good. Now go to sleep, no dinner for you today!" was his order for that night as he retired to his bedroom.

Didi silently tucked me into bed and tried to comfort me as I cried myself to sleep that night, wishing my mother was around to help me and fight with papa when he was being cruel.

Once in a while, when papa was in one of his rare chatty moods, he would ask me to come sit by his side and look at his engineering drawings. Most of the time the drawings would be about the different views of the canal or some improvements to his interlocking tile design or the effort involved in keeping the canal straight and both the sides parallel throughout the length. He cared deeply about the canal being strong and expected it to last hundreds of years.

As a kid, I thought all that was boring stuff and never gave much regard to anything past that minute. But whenever he spoke of his engineering and science stuff, he was the most gentle and kind towards me, and that is why I liked it whenever he was in such a mood. There were times he would reminisce about the one month he spent in East Germany as part of his visit to the Soviet Union during his engineering college days. Although he had gone to study dam and canal construction in East Germany, it was the town layout and the roads and streets of the place surrounding the Eibenstock dam that really impressed him.

"You know what was different about the German town?" he would ask, with a glint in his eyes, that of a man who has had a profound revelation.

"I don't know. There was more water and trees? The people were different?" I blurted out with a question as my response.

"Yes, there was more water and trees, and it was not a desert. The people were pretty much the same, but maybe of a different colour. But what was different was that the streets were all in a straight line, and the intersecting streets cut at right angles to form perfect boxes. That made the place look more open and wider, unlike Calcutta where all streets are like rivers meandering about rather than straight lines, making the place seem very closed and crowded," he would excitedly state as if he had seen a magical creature.

That stuff usually put me to sleep and I began yawning. He probably realized that it was a waste talking to me about those things, as I was more interested in pulling pranks on neighbouring villagers or playing out in the street rather than thinking about his engineering things.

"Come, let's go to bed!" Every night, didi tucked me in and would sleep on the mattress next to me, telling me stories. I loved her stories, they were so much fun and would go on forever and I wouldn't know when I would fall asleep listening to them.

Till I was about ten years old, it was mostly didi and sometimes papa who taught me how to read and write at home. During the daytime, I had a lot of time to myself, as I would be alone at home while didi and other kids were at school or at work in the fields. I would spend most of it reading books.

On days when papa worked late in the evenings, I would gently sneak out past didi's watchful eyes and head out to play with the neighbouring kids on the street. Marbles! That is what I was interested in. They were fascinating with their smooth texture and the colourful glass shapes inside them, and I could use my prosthetic hands to play.

One evening, as I was about to step out onto the street, I took a quick peek to make sure that Somu was nowhere in sight as he would make it a point to pick on me and make me feel miserable. We were playing the game of chaarkoni, where everyone had to hit the centre marble from the corners of a square. If you missed it, then the marble becomes part of the growing jackpot. With each player that missed the mark, the number of marbles in the pot grew and the game continued till someone successfully hits the centre marble.

There I was, having carefully positioned my striking marble at the vertex of the square and about to take aim and hit with my right prosthetic arm, when I suddenly felt a tug on my hand. Then a sudden force lifted me up by that arm, sending a shooting pain through my shoulder as my entire body was hanging by that arm. I was surprised and scared as I stared into the angry face of papa, who was dragging me by my arm towards our house, without regard for my left limb as it grazed the sandy street and the concrete pavement right in front of our door. The other kids scattered before he could shout at them.

As we got into the house, he bolted the door and put me down on the floor, and looked at me with fiery eyes, "What were you doing?" he shouted, as he didn't expect me to while away my time hanging out with those on the street playing silly games.

Hearing the scolding, didi came out from the kitchen. I looked at her sheepishly, as I knew I had sneaked past her and that would get her in trouble as well.

"I told you to keep an eye on your brother. He is always sneaking out and doing everything but studying," he shot at didi. She knew better than to open her mouth.

He put me in that punishment closet again. "Think about what you did wrong and how you are going to change your behaviour. Till I get a satisfactory answer, you will be in that room," he spoke as he closed the closet door on me.

Sometimes, I would passively fight back by not complying to papa's demands. Whenever he asked me, "Have you thought about it?" my reply would be, "I am still thinking!" knowing well that my response would only drive him up the wall and infuriate him further. This was one such time.

My resistance to papa's inquisition went on for a couple of days, which was the longest I had ever been in that closet. I was kind of getting used to it. But didi could not take it anymore. She loved me way too much to have me locked up there forever.

"Papa, why are you keeping Chaitanya locked up?" asked didi with concern in her voice for her poor brother, but also afraid to offend papa or show any disrespect.

"None of your business. You go, study!" Papa responded with finality.

"He has been locked up in that room for two days now. What did he do so wrong that he deserves this punishment for so long?" The pain was clear in her voice and she was about to burst out into tears.

"Wasting his time playing marbles with the street kids, when he should be focusing on reading and studying his subjects," Papa responded with his head buried in canal drawings on his study table.

"All other kids in the village do that, and he needs to take a break as well. You are being too hard on him," she said with tears rolling down her cheeks. I admired her courage.

"Some of those kids were smoking tobacco," he replied, signalling his displeasure for anything frivolous.

"But that is not his fault. I am sure he would never smoke that stuff himself."

"I am not having this discussion with you anymore." He looked at her sternly.

"And the lines he had drawn on the street for their marble games weren't straight, they were not cutting at right angles, and they were not parallel to each other. He knows better than that," he mumbled as if to himself.

"You know, he didn't draw those lines himself. He had to direct the other kids to do so. You never care for him or help him, and all you do is shout at him and punish him." She could not control herself. "He has to crawl for everything, even when his limbs were scratched and bleeding from the hard floor, or the many times he was struggling to climb up his chair or the times when he was late and could not show up for dinner at 7. You hate him because you think he is responsible for mom's death!" she blurted out as her nostrils flared from the anger she felt at the unfair treatment that her little brother had been receiving recently.

That hit him hard. He turned around, and for the first time, raised his hand high up to slap didi. It took him all his self control to stop himself from following through.

"You are so very wrong," he retorted. "He looks at life as all fun and games and silly pranks, but life in the real world is not going to be easy for him. As a father, I will be doing him a huge disservice if I allowed him to grow up with the notion that there will always be somebody out there watching out for him," he carried on as if he could not hold it any longer.

"It pains me to do this, but I want to break and kill all that is soft in him. So that the surviving small part of him that is hard will become his entire personality, so that he learns to hold himself to a tougher and higher standard, learns to embrace the constant battle that life is. And most of all realize that he can never ever quit." Radhika could notice his fists clench as he spoke.

"In life, you are either a warrior or a wimp. Once you make the decision as to which one you are going to be, you stick with it till the end, no matter what. I want both of you to be warriors," he continued slowly as he gained composure.

"While he is growing up, I will make his life at home so hard that everything else in the outside world should feel like a piece of cake for him," he paused as he looked away into the distance. "I don't blame him for anything. I love him way too much for that!" he let out softly as he returned to his normal self.

Radhika thought she saw what looked like tears in papa's eyes. When she looked back, he had returned to his work; she knew that there was not going to be any more talk for the night.

Chapter 2
Hanging Out with Charvakas
(summer of early 1980s)

The summer heat filled me with excitement, as that brought with it the prospect of the summer holidays. Throughout the last day of school, none of the students could really focus on what the teachers were saying as everyone was waiting for the school bell to ring. I reached home with lightning speed as I pedalled away furiously with my prosthetic arms while didi gave my wheelchair a push anytime it got stuck in the sand. That whole day was a blur as all the street kids were outside, jumping, dancing and playing till the sun set.

The night was an unusually hot one with the warm desert wind blowing in from the west, so papa and didi unfurled the window screens made from *khas* roots, and sprayed them with water and soon enough the fragrant smell of khas drenched in water wafted through the room. With that, the temperature in the room started to drop, flooding my mind with the temperatures and humidity of Payradanga, which is where both didi and I were headed out next morning. Every summer, both didi and I went and stayed with our grandma in Payradanga, the town where papa grew up. Grandma had a lovely home, with a large backyard that had a number of fruit trees.

Every morning, her backyard would be littered with feathers of so many different birds that it was like a veritable treasure trove for any kid. Thinking of the smells of amazing sweets from grandma's kitchen, the cacophony of the birds as they returned home to the trees in the backyard to settle down into their nests for the evening, the din of all the cousins as we sat together for dinner, and the scary stories on the rooftop before falling asleep under the dark starry skies, my stomach was filled with butterflies and I could not sleep that night. Didi was also tossing and turning in her bed, and I knew she was also equally excited about the upcoming trip. And of course, there was my playmate, Devyani, who I was looking forward to seeing again much more than ever before.

"Settle down and get some sleep, Chaitu." Didi scolded me gently.

"How can you sleep, didi? All I can think of is the train, the water ponds, grandma's cooking and her backyard and all our cousins," I replied, while turning towards didi and propping myself up in bed.

"Yes. I am also looking forward to that," she said smilingly as her eyes were filled with joy as she thought of those memories.

Papa started me off at the school in Pokhran last year once I turned eleven years old. As I was about to start school, he got me the most wonderful new wheelchair that had pedals at the top, so that I could move by pedalling with my prosthetic arms rather than legs. Once I got used to it, I knew that it was the second most wonderful thing that I had ever received in my life.

"Starting this year, you will be attending the school with Radhika," declared papa.

"Yay! Will be great to have you at school, my naughty brother!" Didi jumped with joy and clapped her hands.

"But I am happy here at home. With didi's teaching, I am already able to read and understand all the books at home. Why do I need to go to school?" I mumbled my resistance, as the anxiety of facing the teachers and new kids at school was the anxiety of facing the teachers and new kid much too greater than the fear of papa's wrath.

"Because, you should develop your brain and use it for something good, rather than loitering in the streets and whiling your time away with those kids," he said sternly.

And it was decided that I would start school that year.

On the first day of school, as we headed towards school, I remember being very anxious and having butterflies in my stomach. That morning anxiety and the unpleasantness associated with going to school did not go away even after I had spent a full year attending school. The school was on the outskirts of Pokhran, and I could easily pedal my way, except for the stretch where we had to cross an abandoned salt field. Didi had to push my wheelchair to help me cross it.

Most of the day at school was a blur, except when it got to mathematics and science. I could understand and even answer some of the questions that the teacher was asking in those subjects. Till those classes came on, I thought that school was not for me. It was only when the teacher started discussing mathematics that I realized that I could participate in the class. It also helped very much to see that the teacher, Ramesh sir, was nice to me and responded positively to my excitement for the subject. Ramesh sir ended up being my favourite teacher for the entirety of my years at school.

"Aye lule, tu school kaise pahunch gaya?" said Somu mockingly from behind me, as the first class ended and the teacher left the classroom. This was the same bully from my street, and my heart skipped a beat when I heard his shrill nasal voice. This was my worst nightmare come true. Oh no, not him, not here!

"This school is for everyone. I am also allowed to attend it," I replied, trying to be as pleasant as I could.

"Oh, the lula speaks. You think the teachers are going to protect you in school? I will show you!" I could feel him trying to approach me from behind based on the direction of his voice and the snickering of his band of cronies, and before he could get hold of me, the next teacher walked into the classroom and saved me. At least for the moment. I didn't want to be in school anymore and missed the comfort of my home, protected by those familiar walls that didn't hurt me or made my life miserable.

While the class was going on, all my focus was on figuring a way out of being bullied by Somu. Maybe I could make friends with Samarjit. He was tall, built like an athlete, and had a group of friends that seemed very loyal to him. He was probably the most popular kid in the school, was an amazing hockey player and the captain of the school hockey team. He was nice and friendly with everyone, didn't seem to be afraid of anyone – including the teachers – and fun just seemed to follow him wherever he went. To my anxious and troubled mind, becoming friends with and joining Samarjit's entourage seemed like the only way to survive at that school.

With that thought in mind, as soon as the teacher got ready to leave, I turned my wheelchair around and started pedalling to get myself to the last bench, where Samarjit was seated. Before

Somu had a chance to react or say anything nasty, I reached the last bench.

I blurted out sheepishly towards Samarjit, "Can I sit here?" as his other mates looked on.

"No," Samarjit said in a flat tone without being mean, something that only he could do.

I did not expect such a blatant refusal. I felt miserable and began pedalling back to my original position and gingerly sat there, hoping not to be picked on by Somu again. Oddly enough, despite that refusal from Samarjit, I didn't feel any anger or resentment towards him. I clearly remember wondering whether that had more to do with his charm or my own ability to not get angry.

"Told you, nobody is going to protect you here, lule," Somu announced with that same prior mocking tone as he approached me from behind and kicked my wheelchair forward.

As I had the wheelchair handbrake on, the push made the wheelchair tip over and I fell on my face. Most of the class burst out in laughter. I was terribly humiliated. I could very well have died right there on that floor, as I didn't feel like getting up and neither did I have the desire to face the class again.

That is when Ramesh sir stepped into the class, set my wheelchair right and asked me to get back into the wheelchair. He didn't try to help me, he didn't show pity on me, and he gave a stern look at the class so that nobody as much as snickered all the while I was trying to get myself back into the chair. At that point, he became my saviour and for that I felt forever indebted.

As the school bell rang, all the kids ran out of the class. I waited for the student traffic to die down before I started pedalling out of the classroom to meet didi on the way back home. Once all the students had cleared the classroom, I slowly started pedalling out, only to see Somu blocking the door and grinning. I wondered as to what kind of sick sadistic joy he derived from terrorizing and scaring me the way he did. Maybe some people are just wired differently from the rest of us. As he came towards me, I raised my prosthetic arms and tried to cover my face and protect myself.

"Stop! Go away! Don't hurt me!" I flapped about my limbs. I could hear didi's voice in the far distance.

"Chaitu, wake up! Wake up! It is time to get up. We have to leave for the train station in two hours. Come on, get ready!" she spoke in that annoying tone that worked better than any alarm clock. I was glad it was just a dream and that Somu wasn't really trying to beat me up.

It was about 9 a.m. when Jagdish arrived in the auto rickshaw at the front door to take us to the train station. Jagdish, who worked on the canal with papa and had become sort of his deputy, volunteered to drop both of us at Payradanga as papa was busy with the construction work. Jagdish was a kind and gentle soul, wearing a colourful Rajasthani turban and sporting a moustache that was curled up in circles at the edges. He was always quick to smile and ready to help us out whenever we asked for it. I liked him because he never made me feel like I was a burden, despite the extra effort required to get me in and out of the train.

Papa waited till the train let out three whistles, and as soon as it started rolling, he left the platform and exited the station as he hated long goodbyes. Others would linger around waving from the platform, but papa was gone after one wave. As for didi and me, we could not be bothered with any of that, because this was the journey we'd been waiting for all year long.

The train journey took us through Jaipur, Delhi, Kanpur, Kolkata and finally to Payradanga, and it took us three trains and over forty hours to reach grandma's place. The time did not matter because every major train station was an absolute delight of snacks or meals, including hot samosas, hot pakoras, fresh boiled peanuts, fresh jamun, figs and other fruits, and meals served at our seats while the train was in motion. Jagdish made sure that we were well fed throughout the journey.

By the time we reached grandma's place in the evening, all three of us were dead tired, and I just wanted to take a long cold bath, have grandma's cooking, and sleep on the soft mattress. The long hours of train ride had messed up my head as the whole ground continued to move under me as if I were still in the train, even when I was going to fall asleep on solid ground. The moment my head hit the pillow, I was out like a bulb.

"Come on silly, wake up! Wake up... wake up," she was sitting next to me on the bed and tapping me on my chest, sprinkling water droplets on my face and doing everything except slapping me to wake me up. There she was, Devyani in her school uniform, as she had just returned from her last day of school and had rushed over to grandma's house to see us.

"Hey Devi, let him sleep," shouted grandma from the kitchen.

"Yeah, he has had a long tiring journey, let him sleep," echoed didi who had already recovered and was all up and about, helping grandma with her cooking in the kitchen.

"He can sleep when he goes back to Pokhran. While he is here, he had better get out and play with me," she kept shaking me, as if both grandma's and didi's admonishments hadn't registered with her at all. We got along so well maybe because she was also about my age, twelve years old, had this bubbly personality and an unstoppable zeal for life that was infectious, and did not really care for conventions or doing what was expected of her. She had boundless energy and my whole being would come alive when I was with her.

Her naughty eyes, her dusky smooth skin, the scent of jasmine from the flowers pinned in her hair and that irresistible smile – despite grogginess, there was no way I could contain myself or stop myself from smiling back.

It was about three years back, when I was nine years old, that we both first met. The first time I saw her, she had a few teeth missing but her smile was the same. Her first question to me then was, "What happened to your hands and legs?" I could tell that she was genuinely curious to find out what had happened to me.

"I was born that way. They say, god made me this way," I replied as a matter of fact, as I had been used to that question from others, but this time around I wanted her to like me despite my imperfections.

"I don't believe in god," she declared looking at me seriously and scanning my face intently to see my reaction to her statement, and within an instant that expression on her face changed back to her usual naughty smile.

"Does it tickle here... or here?" She jumped closer to me and traced her fingers along my body and the ends of my stubs. That was the first time anyone had done that to me, other than didi that is.

"Hehe... hey that tickles." I giggled as I could not control myself.

That is exactly what she did again now, to get me to laugh, and to jolt me out of my slumber.

"OK. I am getting up. I can see that you won't let me sleep," I tried sounding a bit annoyed, but actually I was very glad to see her.

Devyani clapped and said, "Yeah, get up and let's go out. It is time people will be putting out their sigris to get the charcoal fire going before they start cooking for the night!" The tone she took made it clear to me that there was a prank right there that she had in mind, and I better not be late and miss it.

"Ooo hoo, it is good to see that you have a wheelchair, now we can get away even faster than before!" she exclaimed, taking stock of the wheelchair and rolling it around.

"Careful, Chaitu! Don't get carried away and get in trouble," Didi shouted, as I got into the wheelchair and pedalled myself out of grandma's house. Didi knew that Devyani was trouble and she would involve herself and me in some prank or the other, but she also knew that she wouldn't really be able to stop me.

"Stop!" Devyani announced softly, signalling me to stop before we got in front of the line of sight of the house at the end of the street. "This woman treats her stepchildren very badly, never allowing them to play and making them do all the work in the house. Here, take this mug and pour water on her sigri, so that you can put out the fire in the charcoal," she spoke, placing the mug in my prosthetic arms.

Even with my heart beating rapidly for the fear of being caught and being yelled at or worse, I still managed to pour the water on to the sigri and put out the fire, and made my exit from that place as fast as I could. I don't remember pedalling that furiously ever before.

Devyani took me to all the houses around the area where there were women who were mean to either their kids or their families or their guests. It was silly but it didn't matter, as it gave us something to do, and it made us feel like we were doing something good by making the mean ones suffer.

After a couple of hours of running around the neighbourhood, both of us were tired and ready for dinner. As we reached home, I asked grandma, "Can Devyani join us for dinner, Dadi?" I almost begged my grandma, as she preferred to have only family members for dinner with so many cousins staying with her during summer time. Grudgingly she accepted, as this was the first night I had arrived there and she liked to see me happy.

After dinner, Devyani left for her house where she lived with her parents and her grandpa, while I crawled up the steps to the roof of grandma's house which is where we slept during most of the vacation, under the starry dark skies.

My days were filled with waking up in the morning, quickly finishing breakfast and heading out of the house towards Devyani's house, where she would be eagerly getting herself ready to head out as well. It was her grandfather, Charu Dada, who would usually be sitting outside in the rocking chair with the daily newspaper in his hand as he spoke, "Don't go too far, Devi. You know, not everybody is good-natured. Be careful!" He would warn her, as there had been quite a few kidnappings of young girls in the area since the Bangladesh partition. Girls were sold into slavery or marriage to sheikhs in the Middle East.

"Let's go to the river!" Devyani proclaimed. "Everyone will be taking their bath in the river. We can pick up the clothes that they leave on the river banks while they bathe." She smiled devilishly and I just went along. While people would be bathing in the Hooghly river, she would lead the charge and I would follow suit, grabbing their dry clothes that were on the rocks or nearby trees on the river bank and bundling them up and throwing them back into the river, making them all wet. It was probably not the best thing to do, in hindsight, but as a kid it seemed like a lot of fun.

It was right there on the outskirts of Payradanga that summer, that I learnt swimming, all thanks to Devyani.

In the previous years, I would gingerly try to get my body wet in the shallow waters and get a feel of being in water, terribly scared of drowning. One of those afternoons that summer, all of us were seated around a well that was brimming with fresh cool water. Devyani came up from behind me, and without warning, pushed me into the well.

That was all so sudden and unexpected. I was panic stricken and knew that I was going to drown and die. Even while I was scared, I could notice intent focus in her face as she sat there right at the edge of the well, ready to jump in, as she shouted, "Hold your breath! No matter what, don't let out your breath and you will begin to float. Even if your head goes underwater, don't panic, just hold your breath in," she kept shouting as I started to drown.

This was not the first time she had done such a thing. In previous instances when she pushed me into a pond, they were mostly shallow where I could rest my body on the bottom and still stick my head out. But in this well, the water was way too deep and I was really scared. But I also had absolute trust in her words, and held my breath in. After a few seconds, once I gathered my wits and stopped madly flailing my body, I began to float. Suddenly I realized that I was no longer going down, instead my head was right at the surface of the water and I could pop it up and take a breath.

And that was my crash course to learning swimming. The moment I got the hang of it, I realized true liberation as I could move in the water as well as anybody else. It was ultimate physical freedom.

The two months of summer holidays went by in a flurry of games, pranks, swimming, mangoes, collecting feathers, lazing around in the lush green fields, scary ghost stories and sleeping on the roof under the open skies right next to Devyani, didi, cousins, and other kids from the neighbourhood.

Next morning, we had to get ready to head back to Pokhran. My stomach sank at the thought of getting back to that house, to papa with his constant scowl, and worst of all, those bullies at school.

That evening Devyani's grandfather, Charu Dada, invited me, didi and Devyani to visit him in his fields. As he saw us approaching the fields, he came down from the machaan, a raised platform made out of bamboos which in this case was about a foot above the wet and waterlogged paddy fields.

"Come, wash your hands, and eat this *roti* and *saag* while it is still hot," he signalled, as he spoke, urging us to sit around the *sigri* on which he was baking the *jowar* rotis.

That taste of the hot jowar rotis dipped in the saag with potatoes and tomatoes still lingers on. It was probably one of the best meals of my life. The backdrop of a setting sun, music of crickets and insects in the background, the cuckoo's song in the distance, large dense trees around and the proximity of Devyani etched that memory permanently in my head.

Despite my desire to stay awake and soak in every last bit of the summer holidays and my time there with Devyani, I could barely keep my eyes open as all that playing around in the morning and afternoon had left me tired to the bones. I fell asleep on the machaan under the dark summer skies as Devyani, who was also finally tired, followed suit. Charu Dada and didi stayed on and talked as long as the fire burnt on.

"She is such a happy and naughty kid. Wish she was more aware of the world around her and was careful who she mingled with," Charu Dada told Radhika.

"What do you mean?" Radhika asked with a mix of curiosity and concern.

"We are new to this area. Having moved here only a few years back, not many people know us and so they won't necessarily care to watch out for our kids. Complicating the matters, most people around here think that we are strange because we are *Charvakas* and that makes us different and none of the religious communities here can relate to that," replied Charu Dada as he was trying to light the fire in his tobacco pipe.

"Who are Charvakas?" This was something new for her.

"Charvakas are people who believe that personal experience and perception should be the only source of knowledge. That means anything that can't be directly observed through experience or deduced through logical reasoning, Charvakas do not accept to be true. In some regions we are also known as Brihaspatyas or Lokayatas, as Brihaspati yogi started it," he explained with immense patience as he was glad to have the next generation willing to listen to what he had to say.

"That seems a lot like science and experiments that they teach us at school. Then that should be a very good thing," she stated as a matter of fact.

"Yes, it should be a good thing, but that is not what everyone thinks. That line of thinking puts us at odds with most religious leaders. Making us the target of their fear and hatred," he spoke with resignation in his voice. "It doesn't help matters much that we don't visit the temple or the mosque, and we don't necessarily participate or perform any pious rituals in front of a god or pray to a god, because we don't believe in that," he continued in a dry tone looking far away into the darkness.

"Life would be so much easier if we could just get ourselves to believe in a god, just any god," he could see conflict inherently woven into their very existence.

"Does that mean you don't get to enjoy any of the festivals?" she asked feeling sad for Devyani and other Charvaka kids.

"Anything that is fun is a good thing to do. Having more fun while staying away from pain is one of our core teachings." He smiled as if he was reminded of some good memories.

"You should sleep now. Tomorrow, you have a train to catch," Charu Dada suggested to Radhika as he began adjusting his bed, getting ready to fall asleep himself.

Next day, we were at the Payradanga railway station early in the morning. Didi and I sat at the window seats while Jagdish sat right next to me. On the platform stood grandma, a couple of my cousins, Charu Dada and Devyani. Didi was quite composed and smiling, and if she was sad for leaving, she didn't show it. I, on the other hand, felt a sudden sadness come up on me and turned my head away from the window, as tears started rolling down my cheeks.

"Don't get on the train, Devi. It is about to start moving!"
I heard Charu Dada's voice.

Devyani would have none of that. Once she had decided on doing something, she got it done. Even before Charu Dada could complete his sentence, she had already got into the train as she ran across the train car and came up to me and hugged me tightly and gave me a kiss on my left cheek.

"I will see you here next year." She smiled and ran back out of the train before I could react or say anything at all.

That kiss on the left cheek, right near my ear, sent a jolt of lightning through me. I was no longer sad, I was no longer aware of where I was, and despite the bleak cloudy morning, I felt ecstatic and ready to take on whatever school bullies had to dish out.

"Chaitu is in love! Chaitu is going to marry her!" Didi's voice broke me out of my reverie, once the train had left the platform.

"Didi, stop it!" I was embarrassed that she could see what was going on in my head, and extended my prosthetic arm to smack her on the head as she ducked.

It was a few days since we had arrived back in Pokhran, when we received a letter from Payradanga, from grandma.

Dear Radhika,

The house seems empty after both of you left. Every time you visit me, you bring so much joy and happiness into my life. I get to be with Paramvir through you both. Radhika, you remind me of myself when I was young. You are so mature and understanding beyond your years. And the care and love you shower on your little brother is beyond compare. Chaitanya is truly blessed to have a sister like you. Chaitanya, you have such a bubbly nature and a curiosity to learn and experience life. I hope that you stay that way throughout your life.

I have some very bad news for you. There have been communal riots in nearby villages bordering Bangladesh. Charu Dada and Devyani were visiting a trade fair in those parts when the riots broke out. During the riots, Charu Dada was beaten up and seriously injured, and he died in the hospital the next day. Devyani was kidnapped and the police say that they can't do anything as she was taken across the border to be sold to some sheikh in the Middle East.

It is with a heavy heart and utmost sadness that I write about them. Devyani brought life to any place she went, and I know Chaitanya liked her. He is too young to make sense of this. This will devastate him and I know that you will provide emotional comfort and support to help him through this.

As your grandma, I wish the best for both of you and never wanted to relay such harsh and painful news from around here.

Your loving Grandma

For the next few days, I don't remember getting out of bed, or eating, or even showering. And neither papa nor didi could shake me out of it. It was as if somebody had pushed a shovel into my body and taken out everything of meaning and left just an empty shell behind. I was just numb throughout and there was nothing I could do about it or fix it. Every now and then I would feel this sudden rush to do something, go somewhere, and fix everything back to the way it was just a few weeks back when I was in Payradanga.

"Bad things happen to good people. You don't stop living or start feeling sorry for yourself, just because those things happened to you. Instead of feeling sad, either you come up with a plan to help your friend or you let her go," that was papa's eventual reaction to the news about Charu Dada and Devyani.

Oddly enough, the immediate anger that I felt towards him, for not understanding what I was going through, sobered me up a lot better than any kind words would've done. I knew I had to figure a way out to get Devyani back from wherever she was taken to.

Chapter 3

The Friendly Dacoits
(summers of late 1980s)

It was the first day of school after the summer holidays, and I did not want to go back to school. But staying back at home, lost in thoughts of Devyani was not an option. Also, papa would not allow it. It was a lot easier to face Somu and others than to face the wrath of my father. Didi packed my lunch, helped me get dressed, and pushed me along so that we reached school on time.

Samarjit was seated on the last bench, along with most of his hockey teammates. He had grown even taller during the summer holidays. Somu had become chubbier and looked meaner than before. Halfway through the second period, while the teacher was talking about Indian history and the partition leading to the formation of Pakistan and Bangladesh, my mind drifted to Payradanga and to the large house with a massive kitchen. Devyani was standing right there in tattered clothes with her face turned away from me. And there was a tall, large, burly man seated at the table in the middle of the kitchen, in long flowing overalls with a mean looking scowl on his face, making her do all the chores.

I kept calling out her name, but she wouldn't even look at me. I tried to crawl up and move closer to her, but I did not even budge an inch. I felt two arms clamp around my lower limbs and pin me down tightly to the ground. And I opened my eyes wide to see Somu's face up close, as he was trying to yank me out of my wheelchair. It was then that I realized that the second class period had finished and the teacher had already left the class, and I was the centre of attention for the entire class. At that point, something snapped in me. I realized that I was no longer afraid, and the single thought in my mind was that if I can't deal with bullies like Somu, I can forget about ever rescuing Devyani from wherever she was or from whoever it was that had kidnapped her.

"Thwack! Thwackk!!"

I raised my right prosthetic arm as high as I could and smashed it into Somu's face and head as hard as I could. That caught Somu totally by surprise and he lost his footing and fell to the ground. The entire class burst out in laughter as this was the first time they had seen Somu being thrown to the ground. I wasted no time as I jumped right out of the wheelchair, which I didn't realize I could at such great speed, and positioned myself right on top of Somu's chest and started pummelling him with my prosthetics.

"OK. Stop now!" Samarjit came over from the back benches and picked me up and planted me in my wheelchair.

"I didn't mean to. I don't know what came over me." I was glad that Samarjit finally noticed me, but also embarrassed that I could do something like that.

"You did the right thing. I didn't think you had it in you to stand up for yourself," Samarjit complimented me for doing the right thing and finally standing up for myself. Despite mixed feelings about what I had just done, his words made me feel warm inside.

"You can come sit next to me, if you would like," he said, reflecting back on my earlier request. I was delighted and started to turn my wheelchair to head in that direction.

Somu had recovered his composure by now, and tried to pounce on me again. Before he could reach me, Samarjit stopped Somu with his palm pressed hard against Somu's chest, ready to push him back onto the ground, and said, "You are not getting anywhere near him ever again!"

That was the last time Somu ever bothered me or tried to give me a hard time.

"No concept is ever too difficult or too complex to be understood," Ramesh sir would always say, emphasizing that it is motivation and desire to understand things that limits our ability to gain knowledge.

Contributions made by Indian scientists like Raman, Khorana, Ramakrishnan and others were very important to him and he made sure I understood what those meant in terms of practical applications. In his mind, it was a foregone conclusion that there was nothing more fun and interesting than science and mathematics, and it showed in the way he talked and taught those subjects. His enthusiasm for those subjects was contagious, and discussions with him on those topics certainly made me feel good about myself. I could not only understand those concepts, but also build on them to answer the trick questions he would pose. He would push the bounds of my thinking capabilities and challenge me to develop models for the movements of the stars and planets, and behaviours of sub-atomic particles and elaborate on conceptual theories, including relativity.

"Come join us for the hockey game against the team from Jaipur," Samarjit and his teammates invited me. I was invited to every hockey and cricket game that the school team played, and I gladly joined.

Samarjit had this aura about him that attracted everybody towards him. Girls liked him and the boys were glad to have him as their team captain. Some people are born with good looks, some are born with a sense of humour, some with a caring heart, but it is very rare that all those are combined in one person. There was not a single person who met Samarjit and was not impressed with him. It was probably his ability to see and bring out the best in people.

Rumour had it that he was the son of a dacoit leader in Chambal valley, but nobody mentioned it or talked about it. I didn't care about the rumours as it was enough for me that he was a great friend. Samarjit stayed in a big house in the village with his aunt who used to cook amazing food and took care of him along with two of her own sons. He would invite me over whenever he needed my help with the school work or when I wanted to hide away from my papa.

Finally I felt like I belonged in the school. I was no longer scared or anxious at the thought of going to school. I began to look forward it.

I was fourteen and the summer holidays were about to start. Last couple of years, didi and I had stayed put in Pokhran during summers, as there was no desire to visit Payradanga as grandma had passed away and the memories of Devyani were too painful for me to visit that place again.

So I was thrilled at the thought of getting out of Pokhran and away for the summer, when Samarjit asked me to join him on his summer visit to his parents' place.

"Papa, Samarjit invited me to visit with him during the summer to his parents' place. They live in Kakekapura in Chambal Valley. Can I go with him to stay there for the holidays?" I held my breath, as I didn't want papa to turn down my request.

"Will you be able to manage on your own for the duration of the visit, because didi won't be joining?" he enquired looking at didi, as he made it clear that didi wouldn't be able to travel on this visit.

"Yes. Samarjit is my best friend and he is willing to help when needed. Moreover, I am able to do almost all my daily activities by myself with little or no help from didi." I beamed proudly while didi smiled, responding to the excitement in my voice.

Once papa had given the permission, didi came by and spoke, "Be careful out there. You know that Chambal Valley is considered the land of ruthless robbers and dacoits!"

"I am going to be with Samarjit and his parents. I will be safe," I replied, confident in my friend's ability to protect me.

Didi and Samarjit's aunt were at the Pokhran train station to see us off. The sun had just set over the horizon, casting an orange glow on the faces of the folks waiting on the platform. The seats and the inside of the train were hot. We couldn't wait for the train to start moving, just to get the cool air flowing through.

For a brief moment there, I felt sad for didi as she would have to deal with papa alone. But then I also knew that she was more capable of dealing with papa. As Samarjit started speaking of his time growing up in Kakekapura, I found myself looking forward to meeting Samarjit's parents and going horse riding in the valley with him.

Next day afternoon, as the train approached Kakekapura, it went over the lush green valley through which flowed the Chambal river. The river was trapped by steep rocky cliffs on both sides and was lined with dense trees near its banks. Kakekapura was a small town, almost like Pokhran in terms of heat in the afternoon, but the landscape was filled with rocky peaks and valleys for as far as the eye could see.

"*Safar theek raha, Samarjit*?" Babloo asked Samarjit about how his journey was, as he came by to greet us at the Kakekapura station platform. Babloo was well built, of medium height, with dark, tanned skin, and was in his early twenties. He was quick to smile and had a very open and friendly personality.

"Yes, thanks for coming by," Samarjit replied. "This is Chaitanya, my friend from school," he introduced me to Babloo.

"Glad you could join us," Babloo looked at me and responded. I scanned his face to see any reactions to my strange physical form. There were none, and it was a relief as I didn't want any sympathy or teasing from anyone.

Babloo helped load our suitcases onto the jeep and started driving us towards Samarjit's house.

"Any friend of Samarjit is a friend of mine," he spoke as he shook my prosthetic right arm.

"Rudra Pratap Singh Gujjar, we all respectfully call him 'Dada Saheb', is Samarjit's father and he is also our leader. It is a great honour to be staying at his house and to be his guest," Babloo continued, giving me an interesting glimpse into this side of Samarjit.

"Dada Saheb didn't want Samarjit to be associated with our activities, hence he sent Samarjit off to Pokhran to stay with his sister and study there." He looked at Samarjit and then me, to see if I already knew this about Samarjit.

By the time we reached the house, which looked like a cave from the outside, I picked up from the conversation with Babloo that Dada Saheb was the leader of the dacoit group that continued to operate in the area settling complaints and disputes, delivering justice, and protecting the villagers. That wasn't a total surprise to me as I was half expecting that to be the case based on the rumours that I had heard at school, and some of the conversations between Samarjit and his aunt when I used to visit him at his aunt's place in Pokhran.

"Come, come in!" Samarjit's mother spoke excitedly, inviting us into the house, as she saw us arrive at the door.

"*Kaise ho, Mataji?*" Samarjit touched her feet.

The inside of the cave looked very much like any other house, with tall ceilings made by carving the rock. There were no windows, but it was nice and cool inside, despite the bright hot afternoon sun outside. She opened the doors to a room with two beds, "This will be your room as well," she spoke looking at me.

"Freshen up, and you can come join Babloo for lunch," she spoke to both of us, as she headed back into the kitchen.

We were just about to finish lunch when Babloo said, "Tomorrow afternoon, we have the Kakekapura mela. All the villagers from around the Bhind area will be coming by to meet with Dada Saheb."

The next morning, Samarjit was already awake and was outside, saddling up his horse. It was a white horse with a black nose and lips, silver grey mane and tail, and greyish black spots and patches across the white body. It had glossy skin and seemed to recognize Samarjit, as he seemed playful while Samarjit was patting and scrubbing him.

"Come, ride with me." Samarjit wanted me to get on the horse.

"Don't think I will be able to." I was petrified at the thought of being on the bumpy ride, while holding on with my prosthetic arms.

"I will tie this rope around your waist and have that tied around mine. You will be tightly tied to me and there will be no chance of slipping." He had already thought about it all.

It was an amazing feeling to be riding on the horse and feeling the early morning cool breeze against my face as the horse rushed through the valley.

By afternoon, we made our way to the mela. More than five hundred villagers had gathered in a large flat ground that had a huge banyan tree in the middle of it. Seated under the tree was Dada Saheb and a couple of his comrades. All the villagers had gathered there, because they trusted Dada Saheb's leadership and his sense of fairness and justice. If I thought Samarjit was popular in Pokhran, it was even more so in Kakekapura. Everyone from the villages and in the town seemed to know him, and he knew them as well. My admiration for Samarjit grew even more because of the way he treated everyone with respect and displayed great humility when interacting with them.

One by one, each of the villagers came up to Dada Saheb to ask for either advice for future planning, to settle a dispute, complain about the politicians in the area or money troubles.

To all their queries, Dada Saheb either seemed to have an answer or was going to address it for them in the near future. It was mesmerizing to see the interactions between the villagers and Dada Saheb, and seeing the villagers walk away with a content smile most of the time.

A few days later, we had just finished lunch and it was one of those rare occasions when Dada Saheb did not seem to be rushing out hurriedly somewhere and decided to spend time with us. We gathered under the shade of the banyan tree right near the house.

"Why do you do this, when the police are against you?" I asked Dada Saheb in the softest voice I could muster, thinking about all the dangers they faced.

"Despite how it may seem, I wasn't always like this," Dada Saheb replied in a deep confident voice, as he rested his back against the large trunk of the banyan tree.

"Do you know about the Independence revolutionary, Bhagat Singh?" he asked looking at me and I nodded in acknowledgement.

"The ruling British in India hanged him at the age of twenty-three, by calling him a terrorist. The treatment, by the current Indian government, of dacoits is no different," he spoke and looked around at his comrades, who sat there intently listening to everything he had to. They sat upright with their backs straight as if they were trained military soldiers and reflected in their posture and demeanour the immense respect they had for their leader.

"When India became independent, I was happy beyond anything else. Like every other Indian who had fought for independence and freedom from the British till then. But what followed after that was not freedom for the people of my kingdom." He got off the stone bench and walked forward as he spoke. "This land, its citizens, and their well being were the sole focus of my father's life, Prithvi Raj Singh Gujjar. He and his ancestors treated their citizens in a fair and peaceful manner, allowing full freedom to farmers to grow crops, traders to conduct their trade, craftsmen to pursue their craft, and artists to create and perform art."

"The Jains, the Buddhists, the Parsis, the Muslims, and the Hindus all could flourish, build their places of worship, and pursue their own beliefs. The jewellers, the weavers, and other traders could trade freely and some of them even became richer than the kings, which speaks volumes about the rights of the citizens in this kingdom," he spoke, with deep passion for the religious openness, as he reflected on the past.

"I was twenty-one and had just completed my studies at Oxford College, England, when we gained independence. When Nehru made a push for nationalizing all private land, I was one of the first ones to convince my father to give up land ownership to make the lands of the kingdom become a part of the national lands to be redistributed equitably to the citizens," he spoke with excitement as the events of the past unfolded in front of his mind's eyes.

"What followed after the nationalization of lands was nothing short of ugly," his tone changed into anger.

"The politicians who were in charge of distributing the lands equally among the citizens got greedy. Instead of distributing it to the citizenry, they gave away the lands to their immediate families and their relatives, leaving citizens without any way of making a living, while overnight making beggars out of decent hardworking people." His nostrils swelled with anger and his face turned red as continued.

"I dreamt of a happier and wonderful Bhind and Chambal, but I was so very disappointed!" he punched hard into the trunk of the banyan tree to vent out the anger building in him. For the first time, I could understand that anger as it was born out of similar frustration that I felt when I learnt of what happened to Devyani and my inability to do anything about it.

"Even after the nationalization of lands and the politicians taking over the lands, the people of Bhind would still approach my father and later on myself to render judgement, to solve their issues, and to protect them from on the loan sharks. I had no kingdom and I didn't believe in monarchy, but still the requests from people kept piling up and I could not turn a blind eye or a deaf ear to that."

"The reason why they all kept coming back, the reason why they don't give away our hideouts even when they could collect a big reward, is because they care for the fair treatment, the justice rendered and for the support we provide to them," he continued.

"In all the twenty-five years that I have been doing this, I have never stolen or robbed or killed a good citizen. Only those who were causing harm to others and living off of others' hard work, we went after them and robbed them to give it back to those to whom it rightfully belonged. Neither I nor my comrades keep any of the stolen property for ourselves. And I expect to keep doing this till I die, because I can't think of anything else better to do in life. As for Samarjit, I want him to be away from this while growing up. If he decides to do this work, he will be free to make that decision when he becomes an adult."

As he was about to speak again, the horses started neighing. Babloo came running up and announced that we would have to disperse, as they had spotted a military helicopter headed in our direction. It was clear that they had been through situations like these many times before. They all spread out in different directions, each one knowing where they were supposed to go, without a word being said.

Samarjit got me saddled up right behind him on his horse, and as we rushed out, he gushed out with excitement to have heard

Dada Saheb speak at such great length. "My father must really like you and sees you as capable of understanding all that he had to say. He usually doesn't talk much."

Pranav Yadav, the political leader in the area who had amassed a lot of the nationalized lands that were supposed to be distributed to the people, had escalated the atrocities committed against the poor women in his area because he knew that he could get away with anything. Villagers complained to the police, but to no avail, as the police were pawns in the hands of Pranav Yadav. So the villagers came to Dada Saheb and relayed all that had been going on and the heinous crimes against women in the area by Pranav and his cronies.

Despite the portrayal in the newspapers and magazines of dacoits as unruly lawless robbers and killers, Dada Saheb and his comrades were kind, caring and intelligent men. They never took any action without extensive planning and didn't punish anybody before establishing beyond doubt that the individual is guilty and has been harming those who can't protect themselves.

Samarjit and I were just about finishing our breakfast when Dada Saheb entered the room and declared to Samarjit's mother, "Today we are going to capture Pranav Yadav and his sons, as they are passing through our valley."

"Please be careful. He has all the police in his pocket," Samarjit's mother said in a voice laced with concern.

"We have been planning and waiting for this opportunity for a few months now. We are prepared," Dada Saheb replied and ducked into his weapons room. When he emerged, he had a white shirt on which stood in stark contrast to the large black belt with red bullets strapped across his chest, a double barrel gun slung on his right shoulder, and a sword hanging by his waist.

"*Vijayee ho!*" Samarjit's mother spoke as she placed the red kumkum tika on Dada Saheb's forehead, which made his persona even more formidable.

"Can I join you, Father?" Samarjit asked without a tone of hesitation. I admired that confidence in Samarjit and the utter lack of fear when he addressed his father. Wish I could speak like that and act like that when I faced my papa.

"This is dangerous and it is my battle, not yours. I want you to focus on your school." Dada Saheb spoke looking intently at Samarjit, leaving no room for negotiation.

With those words, Dada Saheb gave a quick hug to Samarjit's mother and stepped out to meet his comrades and he was gone. Samarjit continued to finish his breakfast and I sat there with a thousand emotions running and a sort of unknown fear and excitement building inside me as I gazed at my half eaten breakfast. I was not hungry anymore. I wished I had that courage and the ability to do something similar to protect and bring back Devyani.

Samarjit was equally adamant and brave, but he was never disrespectful of his father. We did not go out to our usual haunts that day, as Samarjit thought it would be careless and unwise of us to do so, while ambush was underway. We waited breathlessly throughout the day, with Samarjit pacing endlessly in the living room of that cave we were in, while I tried to busy myself with my books.

"Knock, knock!" There was a knock at the front door.

Both of us jumped out of our skins as Samarjit rushed to check the door. "Babloo, how did everything go?"

"Everything went as planned. Thank god," Babloo spoke.

"Thank god. *Yug yug jiyo!*" Samarjit's mother blessed him.

"Come, join us for dinner, and tell us all that happened today," Samarjit invited Babloo, curious to find out the details.

"Pranav Yadav and his two sons, Yogesh and Jeevan, were in the white ambassador car positioned between two jeeps with bodyguards armed to the teeth with guns. As that entourage came up to the roadblock we had erected, we could see that the drivers and bodyguards were slightly nervous." Babloo spoke, as we were all ears, intently hanging on to every word he said.

As they tried to reverse and back out, I rolled down a couple more boulders that blocked their exit as well," he continued, beaming with pride at his contribution to the ambush. "They were now blocked from moving forward or back. At that point, Dada Saheb came into view riding his horse and fired a couple of shots in the air. At that signal, all of us came out of our hiding positions," he spoke with continued excitement in his voice. "Did my father say anything at that point?" asked Samarjit, anticipating and trying to predict the events.

"Yes. Dada Saheb spoke out loudly, 'Those who drop their weapons and surrender will not be harmed. Our fight is with Pranav Yadav for the crimes he has been committing against the villagers, and we have no rivalry with anybody else.' His voice rang through the valley. As those words reached those vehicles, we could see a flurry of activity, as the drivers jumped out of their vehicles and prostrated themselves on the ground, signalling complete surrender," Babloo continued. "'We are not in favour of bloodshed. All of you in those two jeeps, surrender now and we will allow safe passage,' Dada Saheb spoke again." None of us could eat or focus on food, as we were completely absorbed in that story that was playing out.

"At that point, the bodyguards threw down their guns and kneeled down on the road right next to the supine drivers, with their hands raised behind their heads, in a sign of surrender, leaving Pranav and his sons to fend for themselves. Dada Saheb's voice thundered to call us, and we all came down the valley on our horses, with our faces covered with our scarves, and circled the white ambassador. Pranav didn't want to surrender and he didn't want to give in. He pulled out a revolver that he had with him in the car and aimed at Dada Saheb and was about to shoot at him, when Dada Saheb shot him before he could pull the trigger." He turned his face away from us as he spoke. It was clear that they did not like hurting people.

"Was it part of the original plan?" Samarjit's mother asked.

"Yes. We all knew and agreed that Pranav will not change his ways and will continue to victimize poor women and the villagers as long as he was alive. He had to be killed, for the people to live in peace." For the first time I could see where Samarjit gets his sense of pride, strength, and above all a sense of fair treatment of those around him.

"What happened to his two sons who were in the car with him?" I asked, somewhat hesitant.

"They are being held in the blind cave," he declared with emphasis on the blind part. "Blind cave is a small cave in the valley, where there is only one entry way to get in and it can be sealed tightly shut with a large boulder from the outside.

There is no way for the people inside to move the boulder or to get out. And this cave has a high ceiling with a small hole at the top through which food can be lowered and we can speak with those being held captive there," he answered, almost anticipating my next question.

"We have been using it as a means of changing criminal minds to convert to good behaviours," he spoke as he looked at my face that was brimming with curiosity. It looked somewhat like my father's locking us up in the closet till we realized our mistake.

"As I understand, you will be holding Yogesh and Jeevan Yadav in that blind cave till they make amends to their criminal ways. Wouldn't it be easier to just kill them rather than trying to change them?" I couldn't believe the words that came out of my mouth.

Samarjit smiled at my boldness and my ruthlessness, attributes that had rubbed off on me by just being in Chambal valley for the past two months. "Father believes that if you kill a criminal politician, another will come in his place and conduct even bigger crimes. As long as the politician is not too far gone or too set in his ways, he can be changed and nudged into focussing on being good in the future," Samarjit explained.

It had been five days since the incident and we were out exploring the place as usual.

"The Yadav brothers will be let out tomorrow," Babloo declared, as we came to a stop in front of his horse.

"Does that mean the blind cave treatment worked?" I asked with disbelief, as I didn't expect the dark cave treatment to really change behaviours.

"We can't tell for sure whether it worked. But we know for certain that they are now fully aware of everything they did that was wrong and that we are watching them, so if they go back to their old ways, they will not escape going through this same treatment all over again," Babloo spoke addressing my lack of faith in their treatment. "I can take you there tomorrow, so that you can watch from a distance if you like. I won't tell Dada Saheb, if you both don't."

So, next morning, both Samarjit and I woke up early, finished our breakfast, and were ready to head out as soon as Babloo arrived at the front door. Dada Saheb had already left and Samarjit's mother didn't suspect anything, as both of us were roaming around the valley for most of my stay there. Babloo took us past the cave entrance and all the way up to the top of the ravine where the ground was flat and there were a few scattered boulders for us to hide behind. He pointed for us to get behind a boulder, from where we had a clear view of the cave entrance.

Shortly thereafter, Dada Saheb and his comrades showed up at the entrance of the blind cave. They were all dressed in white, with red turbans and scarves covering their faces, guns on their shoulder, and each of them astride their horses. The Yadav brothers were slowly led out in the sunlight, with sunken pale faces, and blindfolds to keep the location a secret.

"How are you going to conduct yourself once you get back to your lives?" Dada Saheb asked them.

"We will treat all women with respect and equality. We will not impose ourselves on any women. We will also respect the hard work of villagers and not take away the fruit of their labour from them. Our role as political leaders is to serve the villagers and to bring order and justice to everyone, not fill our own pockets while leaving the villagers poor and destitute," the Yadav brothers spoke in a slow, steady tone and it seemed as if they believed every word of what they were saying, at least at that time.

"What do you think will happen if you get back to your old ways?" Dada Saheb asked.

"We will find ourselves back here in this cave!" they spoke in unison, their voices trembling in fear.

Babloo took them down the ravine blindfolded and left them at the edge of the valley so that they could return to their lives and stop being cruel to the very villagers who they were supposed to help.

We had hardly another week of stay left at Kakekapura before the summer holidays were over and we had to head back to Pokhran. It was a beautiful afternoon, especially under the shade of the large banyan tree. Dada Saheb and Babloo had gone away to settle some grievance at a nearby village.

Samarjit was regaling the rest of the comrades with his stories from his life back at Pokhran while at the same time engaging them to share their fantastic stories and experiences. While he sat there engaging the comrades, it was hard to believe that he was only fifteen. While I could barely gather enough courage to speak to any of those formidable dacoits, Samarjit easily managed to level with them and gain their respect.

"Thwank!" Suddenly a bullet whizzed by and embedded itself into the large trunk of the banyan tree, barely missing Samarjit.

Everyone, except me, knew what happened and knew exactly what to do. Samarjit grabbed me by my shoulder and rushed to his house. He placed me inside the house, while he jumped into the weapons room to grab himself a double barrel gun.

Samarjit's mother tried to stop him, but Samarjit made it clear that with Dada Saheb being away, he had to stop the attackers from getting to the house.

I was scared, both for myself and for Samarjit, as I didn't know what was going on outside the cave. I could hear sporadic shooting and didn't even know who the attackers were. Finally, after an hour or so, one of the comrades came rushing in, carrying Samarjit on his shoulders.

"The police have finally retreated. Samarjit took a bullet and he is bleeding heavily," he said, as he laid Samarjit on the bed.

It was a terrifying and heartbreaking sight for me to see my best friend lying there on the bed, covered in blood. I wanted to do something... anything to help him get better. Samarjit's mother rushed to the bed, to take Samarjit's head and place it in her lap and press her palm on the bullet wound on the right side of his chest.

"Somebody go get a doctor," she called out to the comrades as one of them rushed out to fetch a doctor.

"I am going to be OK, Mataji," Samarjit spoke weakly. Tears kept rolling down my eyes uncontrollably.

It took more than an hour for the doctor to arrive. "He has a collapsed lung and he has severe internal bleeding. He needs to be taken to a hospital immediately and operated upon to stop the internal bleeding," he voiced his medical opinion, while sharing everyone's concern that the closest hospital with an operating room was at least an hour away in Bhind.

"Get the jeep! We are taking him to Bhind," declared Samarjit's mother with a firm resolve and a tone that I had not seen in her before.

The comrades loaded Samarjit up in the back seat of the jeep. It was Samarjit's mother next to him and Samarjit signalled for me to also join him, so they placed me as well in the back seat. I could see him wince with pain as the jeep rolled around along the rocky uneven terrain. Samarjit's mom tried her best to make him comfortable, providing cushion for him in her lap.

"You will have to carry on this fight, Chaitu," he spoke, looking at me.

"Don't say that. We will do this together." My mind could not picture a life without Samarjit in it.

"Although pitaji wanted me to be away from all this, I just can't walk away from this. It is in my blood to help those who can't help themselves. If I don't get through this, promise me that you will continue to do that for me. You are stronger than you think, and you are more capable than anybody I know," he continued looking for my confirmation.

"You have my word," I said, placing my right hand on his shoulder.

Halfway to the hospital, Samarjit lost consciousness and by the time we reached the hospital, he was not breathing anymore. They tried to revive him at the hospital, but it was already too late.

Without Samarjit around, I didn't care as to when I was getting up or sleeping or whether I was eating. None of it seemed to matter. The situation was even harder for Samarjit's mother who had lost her only son. Dada Saheb put on a brave face and went about his activities, maybe because he knew that a lot of the other people depended on him for their well being and happiness.

"I've called your father. He and your sister will be coming to take you back to Pokhran," he told me.

"You are Samarjit's close friend and he liked and respected you. I like you as well. You can count on me if you need any help at any point in your life," he spoke as he hugged me. I couldn't believe the largesse of his heart to be offering to help me out, despite the tragic loss he was experiencing at that time.

I nodded meekly, not knowing what to say and how to deal with the grief that enveloped us so intimately and so suddenly.

On the train back to Pokhran, I hardly spoke to didi. I was utterly lost in thoughts of Samarjit, his confidence, his energy, his ability to fill everyone around him with energy and to push everyone to aim for much more than what they thought they were capable of. I was perfectly capable of living before I met him, but now that I'd known him for a few years, I just could not imagine life without him. When did he become so essential to my existence!

As the train chugged on, I looked out of the window at the green valleys, as the train went past the Chambal river, and wondered whether I had it in me to fight for my own life and to bring back Devyani, leave alone fighting for the weak and the oppressed as Samarjit expected me to.

Chapter 4
Deeper into the Pokhran Nuclear Blast *(1985-1990)*

"Come on! Wake up!" Didi was screaming and shaking me furiously as I barely came about.

"What is going on?" I asked, trying to find out what the anxious excitement was all about.

"The political goons had come around looking for you yesterday, while you were away. It is not safe for you to stay here anymore," she spoke and continued to arrange all my clothes and books in a couple of large suitcases.

"I am not going anywhere leaving you here. Stop packing my things," I protested and tried to block her from going through my things.

"We are taking you to Delhi, from there you are taking a plane to Boston, USA. She was not joking, there was absolute finality in her voice.

"Ramesh sir has been corresponding with Gopal, his friendand professor at MIT University in Boston, during the past couple of months. He was discussing the computer model of the Pokhran nuclear tests you were working on. Given the recent developments, Gopal is willing to accommodate you and help you start your college there at MIT," she spoke. Just then, there was a knock at the door.

"That must be Ramesh sir, here to accompany us on the train to Delhi," she continued, as she went out of the room to open the front door.

"Good morning, Chaitanya," Ramesh sir popped his head in with a smile on his face. "We will go to Delhi and get your US visa formalities completed within the next couple of days. Gopal and a couple of his research students will be there to pick you up at the airport in Boston when you land there," he told me.

"You may not yet realize it, but you have an amazing mind and you can offer a lot to the world. Despite these current setbacks, you have to look towards the future and how you can make this world a better place for everyone. Intelligence and smartness are wasted if they are not put to use for the betterment of humanity," Ramesh sir continued. Such tall talk always left me quite queasy inside as I could never see myself capable of living from one moment to the next. If I really had any such smartness, I should have been able to find and bringback Devyani by now, and also protect those that I loved from harm, including papa and Samarjit.

"I can do all that from here. I don't want to leave Pokhran or didi or you. This is the only place I really know and really feel comfortable in," I protested, looking pleadingly at Ramesh sir, not wanting to go anywhere else.

"It is not safe for you here. They have already murdered papa in cold blood. I don't want to lose you as well. You must leave for US, now!" Didi was choking up in tears as she spoke.

"Who will take care of didi, while I am gone?" I knew didi liked Ramesh sir by the way her eyes lit up every time Ramesh sir joined us at home or while at school. In asking that question aloud, I was hoping that it would be Ramesh sir who would answer it.

"I have a job as a teacher at the school and I have this house to live in. I can take care of myself," Didi spoke, reassuring me.

"I will be around to help her out as well. So you can continue your studies in US without worrying about how we are managing here," Ramesh sir chimed in. Deep in my heart, I hoped that they would decide to marry each other someday, as they both seemed to like each other's company and were united in their passion to teach and improve the lot of people living in that town.

It was a terrible sight to see my papa – someone who had always appeared strong and invincible – lying there on the hospital bed with bandages wrapped around his body and being fed with a food pipe running through his nose.

His last words to me were, "I've had a full and wonderful life, don't ever be sad for me. Remember that the greatest joys in life are found in the service of others. Take care of your didi."

Didi and I held on to each other for the longest time, when papa passed away that night in the hospital. Even though he didn't express his emotions openly and never said a kind word, we both knew that he loved us deeply and he was the bedrock of our family and our strength. With him gone, it was just the two of us in that house and nobody else to fall back on.

In many ways, I felt that I was the one responsible for papa's untimely death. Those political goons went after papa and perpetrated such a brutal and terrible attack on him because he was trying to uncover the truth behind the "Smiling Buddha" nuclear test, that had taken place over sixteen years ago. Although there was no coverage in the media and nothing was admitted to by those behind the test, there was nuclear fallout from the test that had left quite a few newborns and infants, including myself, with disabilities. All papa wanted to do was to get that information out to the public and in the process secure much needed government support and medical help for the affected people.

Jagdish was working with papa that day and he had seen the events unfold right in front of his eyes. Papa and the rest of his team were working out in the field, near the canal, when a jeep packed with political operatives and their goons came up to him. They were armed to their teeth and tried to threaten him and asked him to back down from his stance on the nuclear fallout of the test. Papa was not one to be easily scared and he resisted, at which point they stabbed and beat him up and left him there to die. Jagdish and others in papa's team dropped their work on the canal for the day as they rushed him to the hospital.

The train chugged along towards Delhi, and I kept wondering whether any of this would've happened if I hadn't received that gift from papa at the start of the school this year.

It had been quite a few months since I had returned from my visit to Kakekapura and was unable to get over the loss of Samarjit. I was totally lost and directionless while at school or back at home, when I found this big box with an image of a television and a black pad that looked like a bunch of buttons on it, placed in the centre of my room.

"That is a gift for you!" Papa announced with a big smile. I had never seen him that excited or smile that widely before.

"What is it?" Didi and I were curious.

"It is called a personal computer. It is said that it can do most of the thinking and memorizing that humans can do," he explained, as he started opening the box.

"This must have cost a lot of money," I asked, not knowing how well I could use it.

"Yes. It did cost me my last year's salary, but it will be helpful for you in all the science and mathematics that you do with Ramesh sir. I consulted Ramesh sir and he agreed that this will be useful in your education," he continued as he took the TV like contraption out of the box and placed it on the floor.

For the next few weeks, I was glued to the computer, learning everything it had to offer and understanding the fundamentals of programming and how to use it to do things I had been doing in my head or on a piece of paper. The more I used it, the more I began to love it. Although it was no replacement for Samarjit, it was my closest, next best friend. And I found that time does heals all, even the bottomless pain and hurt from the loss of my friend.

Although I would go to school because papa wanted me to and it would make him happy, I had no desire to go there anymore. Especially with the computer at home, and Ramesh sir visiting home on a regular basis to work with me on it, I had everything I needed at home. Within the next few months, I had already built models of the solar system on the computer that could exactly predict the onset of eclipses and other planetary events. It was amazing to see planetary models play out on the computer screen.

"Why don't you take something more complicated and challenging?" Ramesh sir pushed me to do more.

"Building the planetary model of the solar system was quite complicated having to factor in Newton's laws, interactions of the different planets and the precise astronomical masses and distances," I replied trying to elaborate on the complexity involved in what I had done.

"Maybe something that is equally complex and potentially useful to us," Ramesh sir was mulling something over in his head as he spoke. Whenever he was doing that, his eyebrows would narrow in a frown and he would massage his temples with his fingers.

"Do you have something in mind for me to model?" I asked, looking for a challenge that would please Ramesh sir and papa, because those were the kind of things that really got papa excited and interested in whatever I was doing. Most other times, papa would just come home and bury himself in his work or books and papers.

"How about modelling the "Smiling Buddha" nuclear test we had right here at Pokhran, just a year before you were born?" Ramesh sir asked looking at me intently, without a smile, indicating that he was not joking.

"I don't even know where to begin on that one," I protested, imagining the challenge to be way beyond me.

"Remember, if the scientists who were in charge of the test could do it, then you can do it too," he spoke reassuringly.

It had already become dark outside and papa had just come home from work. Didi burst into the room and announced, "It is dinner time! Let's get going, Chaitu."

"Ramesh, please join us for dinner. Papa and all of us would like it very much if you stayed and had dinner with us," Didi asked Ramesh sir.

At the dinner table, Ramesh sir shared with papa all the computer projects and scientific models that I had created. Ever since the computer arrived in the house, such pleasant moments were a bit more common where papa would ask questions and engage on something that I had been doing. It was made even more pleasant as I worked on those things because I truly enjoyed doing them, rather than working on something just to please papa. In some measure, that work diverted my mind away from missing Devyani and Samarjit.

"Starting today, Chaitanya will be modelling the impact of the 'Smiling Buddha' nuclear test on the computer," Ramesh sir mentioned casually, which made papa abruptly stop eating.

"What will that computer model predict?" Papa asked trying to mask his curiosity, while his tone betrayed it.

"Given all the right parameters and modelling assumptions, the computer should be able to predict whether there was any likelihood of nuclear fallout from the test. Of course, it will also provide the total output of the blast the temperatures at the centre of the blast, and the amount of radioactive material trapped in that crater," Ramesh sir explained.

That level of interest and curiosity from papa was enough for me to get engaged on the task of modelling the nuclear test. It was sheer fun to pull the covers off the nuclear blast that took place right around the time I was born.

"Have you factored the type of the bomb?" Ramesh sir would ask targeted questions, guiding and channelling my thinking and efforts in the proper direction.

"How do I estimate the amount of energy released from a gram of Plutonium?" I asked sounding like a nuclear expert, having learnt more about the bomb in the past few weeks than I had known in all my life. It was surreal to think that the blast happened right in my backyard, just a few kilometres from our house.

Any time I was stuck with building the model and Ramesh sir also didn't have an answer, he would write to his friend who was a professor at one of the big colleges in USA. Over the next few weeks, I would also write letters to Professor Gopal, who was very intelligent and knew everything there is to know about nuclear physics and nuclear bombs.

After weeks of relentless refinements, I believed that the model was ready. Given the type of the bomb, size and type of fissile material, the model would predict the explosive output and the behaviour of the particles at the subatomic level. Finally I was ready to share that model with Ramesh sir.

"Based on my model, the total output of the blast should be thirteen kilotons of TNT," I shared my model and the results with Ramesh sir, as he began to pore over the details in front of him.

"The results of your model are higher than the official accounts as published in the newspapers at that time. The official accounts had it at twelve kilotons of TNT and the international media had it in the range of two to twenty kilotons of TNT," he continued to speak as he inspected the details of the model.

"Let's send the model to Gopal. He can run this against his data and tell us whether what you have built is useful from the point of being able to predict the output of nuclear bombs," he said, finally convincing himself of the details.

In the meanwhile, papa would enquire how things were going on the model. Another first for him – I got to see him waiting in anticipation for the results of something that I was working on. I suddenly felt responsible and knew that my efforts were having an impact on him. I wanted to reveal the details and the results of the model to him, only after I was absolutely certain that it had the correct answers or at least when Ramesh sir believed it was ready for me to share with papa.

"I heard from Gopal today. He thought that your model was really thorough and was able to predict the actual outputs of all the nuclear tests, for which the data was available at MIT data repository, fairly accurately. He thinks you will have a great future at MIT, if you decide to take up your education there," Ramesh sir came up to me at the end of the class at school, when all the students had left and as I was just about wheeling myself out.

"But, how can it be accurate? The model doesn't predict any nuclear fallout escaping out of the nuclear blast during the 'Smiling Buddha' test." I shared my findings with disappointment, as I was trying to get to the final answer that papa cared most about.

"Have you considered the depth at which the bomb was placed in the cellar dug underground?" he asked, trying to make sure that I got all the variables right.

"I had the depth at a hundred feet below the surface," I indicated, as he agreed in agreement.

"What did you model for the type of soil?" he asked.

"Sandy soil throughout," I replied

"Hmm..," he paused, as he pondered further. "We should take input from your father. He will have a better sense of the type of soil at different depths in the area based on his canal engineering efforts," he advised.

That day, Ramesh sir accompanied didi and me all the way home as we returned from school. I could not contain myself, as I was eagerly waiting to ask papa for his input and hoped that the real details of the soil of Pokhran would show that there was in fact nuclear fallout that escaped and made its way to the population around the area. If only I knew the series of events that knowledge would unleash and ultimately lead to papa being murdered so brutally, I would've demolished my computer and the nuclear model right then.

"The soil is sandy till about fifty feet. Below that, it is hard clay for about forty feet, and then it is the rocky core." That night, papa happily provided the details we were missing.

Once we incorporated that into the model, it was clear that the depth was not enough to absorb the full output of the bomb. The hard rocky shell acted as a reflector of the blast, pushing it upwards.

"Yes, there was nuclear fallout from the blast!" I exclaimed as Ramesh sir looked on intently at the flickering computer screen.

Papa was very animated to see the result of my model. His face lit up like someone who had come into light for the very first time.

"Are you really sure?" he asked looking at both Ramesh sir and me.

We both nodded, confirming that we were certain of the results, as we knew that after all the effort that had gone into building the nuclear model, and more importantly after confirming it with Gopal, that the predictions from it were very close to actual outputs.

"I knew it!" Papa pounded the table with the rolled newspaper in his hand, as he got up.

"The scientific team that was behind this test should've known and shared it with the country. The political leadership at that time should've been informed and should've taken measures to clean up the fallout. More importantly the newspapers and the media who covered the blast at that time should've spoken up, as they have a responsibility to state the truth," he continued to pour out his anger and frustration on everyone who was involved with the nuclear test.

"I will write to the chief scientist of that test and share the result of your model. The least they can do is acknowledge it and ensure that those that are affected by the fallout are offered the best medical treatment that is possible in this country," he clenched his fists as he spoke.

Dear Mr. Subramaniyam,

I am in all admiration and awe of the tremendous achievement that your team and you achieved, when you successfully exploded the "Smiling Buddha" nuclear bomb in Pokhran.

The national pride that I felt, when I realized that the tremor we felt on the morning of 18 May 1974 was the result of the successful detonation by your team, was beyond anything I had felt before. I remember speaking proudly of it to my wife the next morning at breakfast when the newspaper announced the details of the test.

Hardly did I know at that time that the test would have a very deep and profound impact on my life.

Because of the nuclear fallout of the test, I lost my wife in childbirth and my son was born with physical disabilities. Based on my conversations with the doctor, Dr. Shubhro Bose from Jaipur, over the last fifteen years, I've gathered that there are other kids born around the same time with various disabilities.

Although none of the official accounts or the newspaper stories at the time mention the nuclear fallout, I have fair degree of confidence based on a computer model that we have developed at Pokhran, and validated by a nuclear professor at MIT University in USA, that nuclear fallout was inevitable, given the shallow nature of the cellar in which the bomb was placed.

In the face of overwhelming physical evidence evident in the children born in that area around that time as well as the computer model based evidence, my request to you is to kindly reassess your findings and declare that there was in fact nuclear fallout.

This will help greatly all those affected by the fallout to receive proper medical treatment and the required financial support from the government.

Sincerely yours,
Paramvir
Chief Engineer, Canal Works Pokhran, Rajasthan

Papa sent off that letter to Subramaniyam Iyengar, who had retired from scientific pursuits and joined the political circles as an elected Member of the Parliament. Maybe he did not want to create any trouble for himself, it was clear that Subramaniyam did not want to acknowledge that there was any nuclear fallout. Finally, after a couple months of wait, papa received a letter from Subramaniyam that left him totally distraught and angrier than I had ever seen him before.

Dear Mr. Paramvir,

I am really sorry to hear of your loss and the physical disabilities faced by your son.

It is unfortunate but it has nothing to do with the nuclear test. We have visual confirmation as well as our own model-based confirmation that there was no nuclear fallout from the explosion.

Sincerely yours,
Subramaniyam

It was at that point that papa decided to publish his own personal story and the results of the computer model with the national newspapers and TV channel. And that is when he started receiving the death threats from local political operatives. Although none of the media channels were willing to print the story, the death threats persisted. Despite our fears for papa's safety, we never thought it would come to this point where papa would be murdered in cold blood for bringing to their attention something that they might have overlooked previously.

"We are here! I will take care of the luggage and you can help Chaitanya off the train," Ramesh sir spoke looking at didi, breaking my train of thought, as the train pulled into the Delhi station.

The next couple of days went by in a flurry of activity as Ramesh sir coordinated with Professor Gopal in the US, to get all the papers in order for us to go to the American Consulate to get my student visa. It was not very common for a fifteen-year-old to be admitted directly to a Ph.D program in the US, with the typical age being around twenty years or older.

"Gopal has promised us that he will be able to take care of you, once you land there," Didi tried to reassure me.

"I am not worried about myself. Wish papa was here to see me off to US. He would have been proud of me, I think." I couldn't hold back my tears remembering him. Although he was never soft or easy to get along with, he was the reason for me to go on and try to give my best. He had shown through his own example that through diligent hard work and focused efforts, one can make an impact on the lives of everyone around him, including his family. Even his last act, right before his death, was to bring justice and fair treatment to those who could not speak for themselves.

"Come along now. If you cry, I will start crying as well," Didi came over to comfort me as we waited at the airport for the plane to start boarding.

"I will write to you every day." I held her tightly for one last time, as I saw Ramesh sir come our way to wheel me to the boarding gate.

"I promise to take care of your didi very well," Ramesh sir tried to address one of my concerns, as I was reluctant to board the flight. "It is the first few months that will be painful, as you adjust to the new place, but once you get settled there, you will be able to come back and visit us much more freely than you currently think possible."

With a heavy heart and tears rolling down my face, I turned away from didi. I knew it was the right thing to do. It was what papa would've wanted me to do.

The airline staff wheeled me in towards my seat and helped me get into my seat. As the plane engines started to hum, I could feel a world of tiredness coming over me and sank into a deep sleep with one phrase that papa used to repeat, and were his last words to me, "It is in the service of others that you will find true joy and happiness."

Chapter 5

Chaitanya Gets to MIT
(1990-2000)

I can't remember the last time I felt as alive and as excited as I felt right then, as I nudged the lever of my motorized wheelchair to get me across the parking lot and over to the curb, as I made my way to the ten-storey building in the downtown business district of Boston. It was a chilly winter morning made extra bright by the morning sunlight reflecting off the snow piled up in mounds across the parking lot and on the sides of the roads. There were barely any trees in the business district and whatever trees dotted the straight gridlike streets were stripped bare of all their leaves by the onset of winter.

John Ratcliffe, in his early forties, over six feet tall with broad shoulders, had served in Iraq as part of the Desert Storm operation, mainly focusing on enemy reconnaissance and surveillance. He didn't look anything like the typical movie-style private investigator that I was expecting him to be. He spoke plainly and told the truth straight to your face. The moment I met him, I knew he was the man for the job. He asked the right questions, had the right skills and tools and access to the intelligence network across the countries to be able to succeed. Right at that moment, I felt it in my bones that if John couldn't find her, nobody else could.

"That was about ten years back, and most of the tracks leading to her would've gone cold by now." John had made it very clear that there was little hope of finding anyone who had gone missing so far back in time.

"You are wasting your money." He wanted me to realize that it was a lost cause.

"I want you to do your best. She is important to me." I had signed him on and paid the retainer amount to get him started on the search, because he was the best and also because he was my only option. I had to believe that he would be successful, as failure just wasn't an option.

Every so often, over the past year since I'd engaged him, I'd get bills from him for the various networks of intelligence operatives he had to involve all across the middle eastern countries. So, when John called up yesterday asking me to come up to his office as he had something important to share, I could not contain myself. He just wasn't the sort of individual who wasted his or anybody else's time.

The security guy in the ground floor lobby of the building checked my appointment and directed me to the elevators that took to me to John's office on the eighth floor. Although I was early for my appointment, his secretary ushered me into his office and got me settled inside.

John's desk was impeccable with only a notebook at its centre, couple of pens to the right of the notebook, a black phone to the left and a tray with a few folders close to the right edge of the table. His table reflected his super focused and uncluttered mind. And in many ways he reminded me of papa, in his reserved demeanour, in his compassionate heart and most importantly, in his tough never say die attitude.

The room had glass windows that stretched from ceiling to floor providing unhindered views of the Boston downtown and the blue waters of the Massachusetts Bay. The wall was filled with photos of John with his Iraq comrades and awards from his service in the military. Other than those accolades on the wall and the table in the centre, the rest of his office was quite spartan with nothing in it that wasn't functional. One only had to take just a single peak in his office to be able to know that there was nothing frivolous about this man. Everything he did had a well-thought-out plan and a clear purpose. And the more I got to know him, the more I liked him.

I straightened up and braced myself, as I heard a couple of knocks on the door. John came through those mahogany doors and seated himself in his chair with a smile, cutting out all the perfunctory pleasantries most folks indulge in. I couldn't wait for him to get to the meat of the matter.

"I have good news for you. Actually very good news!" He exclaimed, recognizing that I was bursting at my seams trying to find out what he had for me.

"Have you found her? Where is she? How is she?" I couldn't believe that I would ever be at this juncture trying to connect back with the only love of my life.

"Is this her?" he asked as he spread out six inch by six inch photos of a woman clad in a black hijab. Couple of those photos had a close up of her face with those same unmistakable naughty eyes, the straight sleek nose and the beautiful lips ready to break into a smile any time. She appeared a lot older than she really was, but it was definitely her.

"Yes, it is her." I still could not believe my eyes that it was Devyani in those photos.

"She is in Abu Dhabi. One of my operatives in that area is waiting for your confirmation to make contact. If all goes well, he might be able to arrange for a phone call for you to speak he might be able to arrange for a phone call for you to speak with her, assuming she agrees to take the call." John sat back in his chair, picked up the telephone receiver in his hands and waited for my signal.

This was beyond my wildest dreams, to be able to find out not only that she was alive and well, but also where she currently was and to be able to speak with her on the same day. With my heart thumping away with anticipation and my mind exploding with excitement, I nodded my consent to make contact with Devyani.

John dialled his Abu Dhabi contact and spoke briefly, hung up the phone, and turned to me as he spoke. "Wait here in the office for the next three hours. The only time she is by herself is when she goes shopping for groceries in the central market on Saturday evenings, and we will try to get on the phone line once she arrives at the market today."

John's secretary came by and escorted me to a waiting room, equipped with a large television set, a telephone, and even more amazing views of the Boston harbour than could be seen from John's office. But my mind was in no position to register any of that, as I anxiously waited, rolling forward and backwards in my wheelchair, for the phone to ring. My thoughts inevitably went back to where my life story had changed so drastically.

I was jolted out of my deep sleep, as the captain's voice rang out over the speakers announcing the approach to Boston

Logan international airport, and as the whole plane shook and shuddered as its wheels touched the ground upon landing at the airport. My heart sank as there was a moment of panic that I was a million miles away from Pokhran, from didi, from Ramesh sir and everything that I have known all my life. Except for the infrequent correspondence with Professor Gopal, I didn't know anybody here. I just wanted to turn right back around and return home, even though I knew how silly that thought was.

The panic subsided and the memories of India and Pokhran receded in the background as I managed my way, guided by the airline staff that helped navigate my wheelchair and myself, through the immigration and customs processing at the airport and saw two young men in their early twenties, holding a placard with my name on it. Despite their unconventional looks with long hair and tattoos, their welcoming smiles and relaxed demeanour put me totally at ease.

"We will take care of him from here," Krishna spoke to the airline staff in an American accent, at least an accent that was very different from what I was used to in India.

"I can pedal it myself. Thank you," I spoke, not intending to be a burden to anyone.

"Dude, we got you. I am Krishna. Nice to meet you and welcome to America!" spoke Krishna with a big smile that made me smile as well, as he got behind my wheelchair. Krishna was a Master's student working with Professor Gopal. Although he was born in America, his parents had emigrated there from India. All the way from the airport to the University, he kept the conversation going and I found myself smiling and laughing at all the things he had to say. I realized that it was not necessarily what he was saying, but the way he said those things and his attitude that brought that kind of positivity and energy to any setting he was in.

"I am Rob. Nice to meet you, Chaitanya." Rob had a very different accent, different from Krishna's. Rob was from Louisiana, and was a research student of Professor Gopal as well. Rob was more contemplative and barely spoke anything on the way to the hostel or the dorms, as they called it.

"How old are you?" Krishna asked, as he helped me into the car while Rob kept the engine running as they pulled the car up close to the airport gate for me to get in, without having to pedal all the way out to the parking lot.

"Sixteen," I spoke, not knowing how they'd react to my age.

"Dude, you are really a baby. You can't even drink alcohol yet then." He laughed at my reaction. The thought of drinking alcohol had never crossed my mind. I was here to go to college and study and make papa proud. That was the only thought that was on my mind.

Along the way, Krishna turned on loud music in the car, and he would turn back and ask whether I had heard that song. Other than the occasional Hindi music that played on the neighbours' radios across the street in Pokhran, I hadn't listened to any other music. It was my first introduction to American music and for that moment, I was really glad that Krishna had come to pick me up. This was the first time since papa was gone that I found myself smiling again.

In under an hour, we arrived at the dorm. Rob stopped the car right in front of the main door of the dorm, and both of them came around to help me out. I turned down their offer for help, as I was determined to make myself physically independent so that nobody had to help me move around the college campus.

"I am going to be your roommate. That is going to be your bed. Anything you need at any time, just let me know," Rob said pointing at a bed in the room as we entered it.

As I would come to know later, although it was just like any other building or room in America, for me it seemed like something from the future. The bed was so very soft and comfortable, the room was fully sealed with complete temperature control and the lines in the room were all straight and parallel at the ceiling, the floor, the windows and the doors. Papa would've been happy living in a room like this and maybe this what he had noticed on his trip to East Germany, that he used to speak so fondly of.

"Once you get settled in, you should give this motorized wheelchair a spin. Professor Gopal ordered that for you, so that you can move about on your own in the University campus," Krishna spoke, pointing at a beautiful, black wheelchair that seemed to have a comfortable leather seat and leather handles with a single lever on the right to move it around.

"Remember to charge it every night. Then you can use it throughout the day," he continued.

That wheelchair was my answer to being totally independent. In my heart and when I first met Professor Gopal, I couldn't thank him enough for thinking about my needs even before I had arrived there.

"Dude, wake up! You have been asleep for more than twenty-four hours," Krishna sprinkled cold water on my face, as Rob had tried to wake me up unsuccessfully already. I was groggy as I barely came about.

"That is jet lag making you sleepy. Let's get you something to eat and also basic stationery from the college store," he continued as he paced around the room.

There were a couple of hours left for the sun to go down when we got out of the dorm. That campus was like a heaven for me, as every difficulty that I would otherwise face due to my physical disabilities was already taken care of. All the pathways had the provision for the wheelchair to get on and get off at the intersections of streets and all the buildings had ramps for the wheelchair to gain access. I was amazed at the thought that had been put into every single aspect of the campus layout. Once I moved out of the campus, I realized that the same thought was placed in the design of the towns and the buildings as well to make everything accessible to those who were physically challenged.

Fall had just set in, with most tree leaves turning all shades of brown, red and yellow as the trees got ready for winter. Coming from Pokhran, where it was scorching heat and sand all around as far as the eye could see, it was amazing to see lush green lawns in the campus which were for the moment covered with heaps and heaps of brown leaves that had fallen off the trees. As we passed one of the parks, it was fun to watch kids roll in the leaves and throw them up in the air and bury themselves in it. The roads were clean, intersected at perfect right angles, and the traffic moved about with cars following each other in what seemed like a perfect queue with everyone waiting their turn.

"What would you like to eat?" Krishna asked as we arrived at a group of restaurants near the MIT campus.

"Anything spicy would do." My mouth watered at the thought of having some mirchi-loaded daal baati or bajra roti, that I had taken for granted so far in my life.

"Mexican food is probably the closest you will get to spicy food in this neighbourhood. Want to give that a try?" Krishna asked looking at both Rob and me.

It was sheer torture to go through the multiple options as the girl on the other side of the counter kept asking, "Do you want hot or mild salsa? Cheese or no cheese? Brown or black or pinto beans." Things were so much simpler back in Pokhran, I just asked for one thing and most times I didn't even have the option as there was just one dish around.

"For here or to go?" She pounced that last question on me as I reach the end counter.

"Err…" I fumbled trying to find out what was expected of me as I tried to answer as best as I could, "I will eat here and then I go." That response left the girl at the counter confused while Krishna and Rob both burst out laughing.

"For here," he answered the girl at the counter, as he paid for our order, while continuing his rambunctious laughter.

"Glad to be of amusement to you," I tried to recover my composure and dignity, and started laughing with Krishna and Rob.

"Gopal sir, thank you very much, for all that you've done for me and for the motorized wheelchair," I blurted out as I first met Professor Gopal.

"Call me Gopal. You deserve to be here for the detailed thought and effort you've put into developing the computer model for nuclear bombs. All the other things are just accompaniments to make sure you can focus on learning. Think nothing of it," Professor Gopal spoke as he shook my hand.

In some aspects, Professor Gopal was like Ramesh sir, as both of them were thin and about the same height at five feet ten inches and had thin fine noses. Ramesh sir had a weather-beaten face more suited to the heat of Pokhran while Gopal's face, with nicely styled grey hair, seemed to belong in an air conditioned library surrounded by wooden shelves and volumes of old books. He always had a blazer on, a woollen scarf around his neck and a fine watch on his wrist.

"Always get to the root cause of the problem at hand," Gopal would emphasize. "As researchers and scientists, it is your responsibility to continue to ask the questions till you've stripped the problem to its core fundamentals."

Ramesh sir, maybe because of where his roots were, focused more on learning what had already been discovered, whereas Gopal focused on discovering and creating new insights and information. To be working with such a professor was both intimidating and exciting.

"Once you get your bearings in this place, I want you to come visit me in our computer lab. We can begin to work on your model to refine it so that it can work for all situations," Gopal came by at the end of his class, and laid out my learning focus for the first year of my college there.

I was particular about taking time out to write to didi. She was my emotional anchor and my guiding light through troubled times. With her being so far away and not being able to speak, letters were the only way for me to communicate. Once I wrote and posted the letter to her, it would fill me up with renewed hope and energy to carry on till her reply arrived in mail.

Dear Didi,

I have finally settled down in this new place. I miss you terribly and wish you were here with me. You would've liked it here a lot. You know, girls and boys are treated equally here, and girls don't seem to think a lot about what they have to wear and whether they will get teased or not depending on what they wear. Something that you would worry about back there.

My motorized wheelchair gets me to all the places around the college and back to my room, without any trouble. Also there is a nurse who comes in the morning for an hour to help me get ready. I don't believe I need her anymore, as I am fully self-sufficient here.

Professor Gopal has been great with everything. While working with him on the computer model, we both seem to lose track of time. Krishna and Rob have also taken interest in the model and are helping out wherever there is more programming to be done to make it more useful.

Krishna is such an optimist and always sees the bright side of everything. Nobody can be down or depressed with him around. Rob is a brilliant physicist and seems like a hopeless romantic. Almost every month he goes back to his hometown of New Orleans, and comes back convinced that he has met the love of his life. By the next visit, that love would be gone, replaced by another. But he never gives up on love. It is when he talks about his love stories that I am reminded of Devyani the most. I don't even know whether she is alive, but my mind can only think of her and no one else.

How is Ramesh sir? Convey my regards and thank him on my behalf for all that he has done to get me here.

Your brother,
Chaitu

It would take three to four weeks, which felt like an eternity, before I got a response. Almost every day after classes ended, I'd stop by the post office to check my mail box. Days when there was any mail from didi were the happiest of all.

Dear Chaitu,

I have good news that I am sure will make you happy. Ramesh wanted to get your permission before asking for my hand in marriage.

You can call me over phone now, as there is a telephone line recently installed at the school.

Looking forward to speaking with you.

Your loving sister,
Didi

Finally, Ramesh sir wanted to propose to didi. The two people I really cared for in this life, were ready to get married. I was filled with absolute joy. That was the first time I called didi and Ramesh sir over the phone line since I'd landed in America. To be able to hear that didi was getting married and Ramesh sir would be taking care of her in future was such a comforting feeling.

"Lockheed Martin, one of the largest defence contractors in America, is interested in purchasing the rights to your computer model for nuclear bombs. All the work that you've put into it over the past four years, along with Krishna and Rob, has turned it into a very useful tool. Do you want me to continue the dialogue with them?" Gopal asked me.

"I will go along with your advice and guidance on that. What do they want to do with it?" I asked, trying to find out more. I was beyond belief that something I'd taken up as a hobby, and to please papa and Ramesh sir, would be perceived as useful to a large corporation where they'd be willing to pay money to buy it.

"They want to commercialize it and sell it more broadly," Gopal continued to gauge my level of interest in that proposal.

"Does that mean there will be more nuclear explosions across the world?" I tried to understand the impact of this decision, not wanting to add to the chaos and destruction in the world. Papa always believed that happiness is only to be found in the service of others, and that is where I knew I would find my happiness as well.

"Nobody can predict the future and how countries will deal with nuclear power. But, commercializing your nuclear model will help armies model the impact of bombs more readily on computers through virtual or digital means rather than exploding real bombs. So I would think that it should make the world safer than it would be without your model," he provided his view on the potential sale.

"Can I think about it a bit and get back to you?" I asked, wanting some time to discuss my very first important decision with didi and Ramesh sir.

"Why not! It is your decision, please take your time." Gopal was very understanding.

When I got back to my room, I called up Pokhran school to speak with didi. Both didi and Ramesh sir thought it was the right thing to do, to sell my computer model to the defence contractor, as it would allow greater visibility and use for what we had developed. Ramesh sir agreed with Gopal's view that having Lockheed Martin commercialize the software model would certainly help the world, or at least not make it any worse than it already was.

The next day, I relayed my decision to Gopal, while Krishna and Rob waited eagerly to know my decision. "I spoke with both Ramesh sir and my sister. They are in favour of selling the model. I am OK with moving forward and selling the model to Lockheed Martin."

"Congratulations! Based on what Lockheed has offered, you get to make ten million dollars, and both Krishna and Rob make a couple of million dollars each," Gopal announced. That was more money than I had any use for in my life.

"Dude, you are awesome!" Krishna hugged me and picked me out of my wheelchair as he jumped around with joy.

Rob broke out of his contemplative and measured stance, and was jumping around with an opened champagne bottle with champagne spilling out onto the floor. He poured all of us some of that champagne, which was my very first taste of alcohol at the age of twenty.

Once the celebrations ended, my first order of business was to send enough money to didi and Ramesh sir, so that they could purchase a comfortable house anywhere they wanted. And the next stop after that was to engage John Ratcliffe to track the whereabouts of Devyani, because at long last, I had enough money to take up that pursuit. In fact, I had more money than I had use for.

'Knock, knock!' I turned around to see John entering the room as I waited for the phone call.

"My secretary is patching the call to this room. You probably have fifteen or twenty minutes at best before Devyani will have to head back," John indicated, so that I could make the most out of the phone call.

Right then, the phone started ringing. I moved myself closer to the end of the table to turn on the phone speaker and waited for John to close the door behind him as he cleared out of the room.

"Hello, is that really you, Chaitu?" It was the same unmistakable voice from a distant past. It had matured since then and sounded a bit more reserved than she did earlier.

"Hi Devi! It is me, Chaitu." I could not control my happiness.

"I never thought I would ever be speaking with you or anyone from my past life in Payradanga," Devyani broke down and started crying uncontrollably. I wasn't doing much better at my end either. How I wished we could hug, but then I was glad that I could at least see her.

"How is my grandpa?" she finally asked regaining composure.

"He succumbed to the injuries and passed away a couple of days after you were kidnapped," I tried to stay as brave as I could.

There was a long pause, and she spoke again, "Thank you for searching for me. It has been close to ten years and I thought everyone must've given up on me. Why did you not?"

"I just could not get you out of my mind. It was the way I felt when I was with you, learning to swim with you, pulling pranks all around, and I can still remember your kiss on my right cheek to this day as if it was yesterday."

"That was so long ago, Chaitu. I am no longer the same." She was sobbing.

"It does not matter. I still love you and want you in my life," I implored.

"I can't be with you. I have two sons and I love them. They are my life now." She got her normal voice back as she returned to her reality.

"So what, you can still be with me along with your two sons." I was prepared to face anything to be with her, as long as she was willing.

"It is not that simple. My sons need their father and I need to be here with them," she continued.

"I can come, stay there in Abu Dhabi, just to be able to see you." Nothing else mattered to me more.

"No. I don't want you to come here, and I don't want you to wait for me. I loved you as a kid, way back. But now that is no more." She was certain that she was never leaving her life there.

"At least tell me that you are happy. I need to hear that." It would have broken my heart to hear anything else.

"I am as happy as can be. I don't love my husband, I don't have much freedom, but I love my sons and have made a life here taking care of them. I have to go now." With those words, she hung up and was gone. Leaving me to move forward to a life without Devyani in it.

Throughout my childhood, didi was my rock and my support in moments of distress. She would prop me up, comfort me and help me make some sense of life each time things crumbled around me. With the hope of being with Devyani completely lost, I was once again at the altar of hopelessness and despair.

Dear Didi,

I finally got to track down the whereabouts of Devyani and managed to speak with her over the phone. She is in Abu Dhabi and doing as well as she can, given the forced circumstances in which she was taken there. I thought once I got to connect with her, I'd be able to bring her over to America or go stay with her. But she doesn't want either of that. She has two kids now and has decided to carry on with the life she has found herself in, there.

Although at first I was disappointed and angry that she would not consider joining me, I see her point of view. I am angry at the circumstances that got us here.

As Professor Gopal says, "Always get to the root cause of the problem," my mind keeps digging into each of these painful events and trying to find the root causes behind each of those. Those thoughts just don't let up, whether I am awake or trying to fall asleep.

Kidnapping of Devyani would not have happened in the first place had they not been displaced from Cooch Behar where they were well established. It was the bad practice of giving licenses to select few that cut off their family's livelihood and forced them to move from their original place.

Samarjit would not have been shot at as an outlaw and a dacoit, had the task of distributing the nationalized lands not been botched by the government. Dada Saheb would not have had to take up protecting the interests of the poor, if the land was properly distributed to all instead of being grabbed by the local politicians.

I would not be seeking revenge on Subramaniyam and his party operatives for murdering papa had the media done its job properly. They are supposed to report on the basis of facts, and had they done so about the nuclear test in the first place, papa would still be alive.

Your brother,
Chaitu

I didn't post that letter to didi, because I just didn't see a point to it. In the service of others, even if I wanted to fix or change any one of those things, I didn't know where to begin or how to bring about that change.

I chalked those up to be the meaningless ramblings of a helpless mind that suddenly found itself at yet another juncture, brought there by circumstances beyond my control, that took away things that I held precious and dear to my heart. Despite my inability to fix those problems or to address the root causes behind those events, my mind could not help going over and over and over again as to how those could have been avoided or prevented from happening again.

Chapter 6

Meeting Zara

(2000-2010)

"Did you notice that? The way she was all chirpy and full of smiles earlier, with that white customer, and the moment you showed up, she stopped smiling!" the girl exclaimed, with a coffee cup in her hand, a wide-eyed expression on her face. She was in her early twenties in torn blue jeans, white t-shirt, a red unzipped hoodie and sneakers. That is how I met Zara Kalash, in the checkout queue of a grocery store in Cambridge township.

"Moreover, how dare she put up a 'lane closed' sign while you were still waiting in the queue!" she raised her voice and demanded to see the manager of the store to complain about the behaviour of the woman at the checkout counter in that grocery store.

I sort of realized where she was coming from, but never in a million years would I have spoken up against such an unfriendly gesture of the checkout staff.

"That is overt discrimination," she continued.
"No, don't go away from the queue. She has to serve you and complete your checkout before she can close this checkout lane," she came up to me and stood in front me, as I was trying to wheel away from that lane towards another open lane, not wanting to draw attention to myself.

But that girl would not have any of that and she was not going to give up until I was treated fairly. She made sure that the same woman helped me out with my groceries, and this time with a smile.

"Hi, I am Zara. And thank you for going along with me on my personal crusade to address discrimination at the checkout lanes in America," she came up to me with a bright smile. Her brown eyes were sparkling and she shook my hand as I was wheeling myself out of the store with my groceries.

"Hi, I am Chaitanya. I wouldn't have been able to do what you just did for me. Thank you," I replied as I'd been too conscious of myself to pay attention to such subtle and passive aggressive forms of discrimination.

"Oh, you attend MIT as well?" she asked as she noticed the red MIT letters on the back of my wheelchair.

"I teach computer programming at MIT," I replied as we headed in the direction of the parking lot where my taxi was waiting for me.

"You don't look old enough to be a professor." She seemed surprised.

"Don't be deceived by my boyish looks and charm. I could be a lot older." I tried to be funny.

"Ha ha," she deflated my attempt as she approached her car.

"You must be smart then," she spoke with a genuine smile as she unlocked her car.

"Not sure about smartness. I may not look it, but I am thirty and just happened to have completed my doctorate a bit early."

I had never thought too much about other students' comments about my looks.

"What are you doing at MIT?" I tried to extend the conversation. Although I had only known her for a few minutes, there was something about the way I felt in her company, that I wanted the conversation to go on into the night.

"Master's in journalism with a minor in urban planning. Maybe we will run into each other on the campus sometime,"
Zara spoke as she ducked into her car.

I didn't have any bright thoughts or conversation lines that would stop her from driving away. As I wheeled away towards my waiting taxi, I had a big smile thinking about the whole series of events in the grocery store.

The taxi sped towards home and my mind flowed back to Devyani, and there was suddenly no other thought of anybody else for me in this life. It didn't matter that Devyani would never be with me; my mind was just not open to any other possibilities.

"Dude, do you need help with the groceries?" Rob asked as I made my way into my house. Krishna and Rob would check themselves into my house whenever they felt like getting away from their families. Of late, we had started partnering on a new project to aggregate personality profiles of people based on their posts on the internet across multiple outlets, including blogs, the emerging field of social media, comments on various websites and their likes or dislikes. With the vast amounts of data available on the internet, it presented an interesting problem for my mind to focus on.

"No, I am good. Let me park these in the kitchen and I will come join you," I wheeled myself to the kitchen to drop off the groceries and returned to my computer.

"You know we got access to the data feedback from this *myspace* network," Rob exclaimed as he received an email from the data manager at *myspace* that we'd been chasing for a while. The sheer joy of building a massive repository of all the people on the internet and being able to tell about their preference was an inexorable drive that propelled the three of us to spend countless hours building a social media preference gathering tool.

It was a warm and breezy spring evening as I headed back from the campus. On my way home, I stopped by the mailbox to pick up mail that I hadn't got to in the last week or so. The MIT magazine caught my eye, with one of the headlines on the cover page screaming boldly,

"Covert Discrimination — can we ever get rid of it?"

As I turned the pages of the magazine, I landed on the article matching that headline on the front page.

Growing up in Karabash (Qerebaş), Syria, as a Yazidi, I had faced discrimination and persecution because of my religious beliefs which differed from Islam. My family had emigrated from Iraq to escape tyranny and suppression under the Saddam Hussein regime in the late 1980s. Conditions in Syria were significantly better as Karabash was a predominantly Yazidi village with full autonomy. As long as there was a stable government in Syria, we could go on with our lives farming and herding sheep and goats. Although we were a minority, we didn't feel inferior to anyone. We were just different in our belief systems and didn't consider ourselves either superior or inferior to the rest of the Syrian population, which is predominantly Muslim or Christian.

When we were first granted visa as a refugee to travel to America, my family was thrilled and I was excited as well. I am glad a country like America exists in the world to provide safe haven to the persecuted and the oppressed, and to those without a voice of their own. So, for the first few years I was in America, I was very happy and felt free to pursue my dreams and do things as I wished without fear of persecution. It was only after a few years of living here, did I begin to notice the subtle discrimination that I or my other Yazidi friends, with relatively darker skin, would face. It was never overt. Nobody ever denied us service or turned us down in an official setting; it was the subtle body language or the rolling of the eyes that conveyed so much more as if we were not wanted here.

Assuming humans will always have an innate need to discriminate, whether it is based on the colour of the skin or the religious beliefs or the level of education or individual wealth, it is an interesting question to ponder whether it is better for such discrimination to be overt or covert.

If it is overt, one can fight it or not engage with the antagonizing community. But if it is covert, it makes every member of the discriminated community fall into the trap of being stereotyped. Actions or qualities of one Yazidi will be used to judge the rest of the Yazidi population. If one Yazidi doesn't tip at a restaurant, then it will be applied to all Yazidis being regarded as bad tippers, or if one Yazidi commits a crime then all Yazidi will be labelled as criminals. It is no different from calling a woman a witch in the dark ages. Once a minority group acquires a negative label or a stereotype, then the onus will be on every member of that minority group, whether they had that trait in them or not, to actively demonstrate that they don't fit that label.

Although I am glad to be living a privileged life in America, I don't feel I am fully accepted here. Maybe it is just the way I feel, maybe it is all in my head. I don't blame the white America for their stereotypes of Yazidis, they are just being human. Any day, I would gladly give up this materially rich life in America to build a small country that is a safe haven for Yazidis and people of all other faiths as long as they are willing to coexist peacefully.

To overcome discrimination in either form, I dream of a time when all the Yazidis gather together to build a new country on their own terms, that will welcome refugees, will provide its citizens full liberty and will defend it vigorously from any enemies of freedom. That will ensure that Yazidis are respected around the globe. If we can't accomplish that, then the only other option is to become a refugee and be discriminated against in whatever country we get awarded asylum – be it in America or Germany or another country. I prefer death to living a life without respect.

Zara Kalash, Chief Editor, MIT campus magazine

I knew right away that this was the Zara from the grocery store from a few months back. There are not that many individuals with such unmistakable passion, force of character and a clear sense of right or wrong. Although, as an immigrant I shared some of those experiences, it was not such an important topic in my mind. I was moved by that article and wanted to commend her on the courage of her convictions and her sense of pride in her Yazidi background.

That night I sent her an email, complimenting her on her article and inviting her to visit my class as I knew that I would be able to help her in her quest for a Yazidi nation, through the technology I was developing with Krishna and Rob, by connecting the dispersed Yazidi community together.

It was a week or so after that email that she showed up at the end of my computer programming class. As all the students disbanded and left the class, she walked up to me from the back of the class, which is where she was seated since she joined the class halfway through my lecture. She was wearing a red dress with her brown long hair forming a mane around her pretty face, and she carried herself with pride and confidence.

"Good to see you, professor with the boyish looks and charm!" her voice rang out from across the classroom as she tried to pick up from our last conversation at the grocery store.

"Ha ha... looks like you have a tremendous memory." I smiled, trying to hide my embarrassment from the first encounter.

"Thank you for your compliments regarding my article," she spoke as she approached my desk at the head of the class.

"I might be able to help you by bringing together most of the Yazidi community that is engaged with the internet in some form or the other. Additionally, I should also be able to help identify all others that are Yazidi sympathizers and those that are anti-Yazidi." I spoke as I started to wheel out of the class. "Would you like to have coffee?" I asked on the way out.

She nodded yes to the coffee, and continued, "How will you do that?"

"Couple of my friends and I have been developing computer programs that sift through mountains of data that is available online and make sense of it to profile people, their preferences, their viewpoints and the level of influence they wield on others. I can point those same programs to help you in your cause." I tried to keep it simple and not slip into computer geek speak.

"And why would you offer to help me? What is in it for you?" she asked, not used to having others make free offers of help.

"You helped me out in the grocery store without expecting anything in return. I'd be very happy if our technology can help unite your Yazidi community and bring about change in their living conditions. This is a completely *pro bono* offer, no strings attached," I replied as I took a sip from the coffee cup, as we steered ourselves into a corner in the campus coffee shop.

"How many Yazidis are connected to the internet currently? Can you tell?" she asked, getting excited about the prospect of connecting with the broader Yazidi community.

"I will have to clean up the data, but there are about four hundred thousand Yazidis on the internet." I opened up my laptop and punched in commands for my program.

"You know, about a century back, we were a community with over twenty million people. With the religious persecution after the Ottoman empire that has continued to the present day, we have been cut down to less than a million people," she spoke, her voice trembling as she tried to rein in her emotions.

"On the bright side, there are more than five million explicit Yazidi sympathizers on the internet," I tried to inject some cheer back into the discussion.

"Really! Can I see who those are?" she came to my side and leaned over to look at my laptop screen. Her proximity, her perfume and the dim lighting of the coffee shop acted like magic on me. My mind could deal with this close interaction with Zara along with thoughts of Devyani without too much conflict. It was a strange and amazing warmth that flooded my entire being just to be sitting there in her presence.

I had to consciously strip myself away from those thoughts and focus on the data on the screen. "Yazidi sympathizers are in many parts of the world, including developed countries that officially accept refugees, like America, Germany, UK and in emerging countries like India that do not necessarily have a clear policy for refugees. Some of the sympathizers in India believe that Yazidism is in some way related to the Hindu religion because of the presence of the Peacock God (Tawsi Melek), the concept of rebirth or reincarnation and the belief in the existence of soul in all living beings, and not just in humans.

"Growing up in Pokhran, a village in India, I was not aware of Yazidis or the hardships that they have had to endure. So it comes as a pleasant surprise to me and as a matter of pride to notice that there are others in my home country that have given it some serious thought and consideration," I continued as I scrolled down the list of sympathizers that our computer tool had aggregated.

"I would like to get in touch with all the four hundred thousand or so Yazidis that your program has picked up. How do I do that?" she asked with childlike enthusiasm.

"It will take some time to extract all their contact details, but it should be possible. Why don't you come over to my house and meet Krishna and Rob, my partners in crime, who have been helping me in developing this program. They are extremely intelligent and fun people to hang out with, and they will also be happy to help you in your quest," I spoke as I knew that this was going to be a long journey of discovery for her and wanted to provide her with all the help she needed. And more importantly, it would allow me to spend more time in the presence of her sunny bright company.

Right then, she looked at her watch and realized that it was pretty late in the night. "Totally lost track of time there. I have a class to attend early in the morning, so have to go now and catch up on some sleep. Would love to meet your friends as well next time."

The moment she was out of my sight, I began missing her. For the longest time, it was Devyani who used to occupy my mind. I didn't think that I'd ever feel that way towards anybody else again, but there I was feeling alive and rejuvenated after that late night encounter in that coffee shop, with this girl in the red dress. Finally, I felt like I could breathe freely again and feel alive again.

It was a cloudy spring morning, with a light drizzle making the whole campus come alive with green lawns and lush green leaves on the trees, a sight that is in stark contrast to the brown dry sands of Pokhran. The representatives from the town of Dunbar, nestled in the mountainous terrain of the Rockies, began strolling into the large glass atrium that was on the top floor of the eleven story building of the MIT architecture department. The sound of the falling rain drops on the glass ceiling acted as soothing background music to the urban planning session that Zara was coordinating.

"Thank you all for joining this town planning session today." Zara was standing at the white board that was at the head of the conference table, dressed in a grey skirt and suit. It was interesting to see a twenty-something student drive the session involving Dunbar town planners.

"I don't have the right answer for Dunbar, at least not yet. Actually, none of us individually have the full answer, but collectively we will develop the right plan for Dunbar's continued expansion," she continued, while moving gracefully across the room, effortlessly making eye contact with everyone seated across the table.

"We have in this room experts in health, water, education, roads, buildings, waste management, energy and transportation. It is with each of your input and creative problem-solving that we will develop a plan for Dunbar that will take into account its rocky mountainous terrain and its unique location," she spoke as she pointed at a map of the town's landscape that was projected on the whiteboard. It was evident from the comfortable way with which she was handling the session that she had done it multiple times before.

It was mesmerizing to see Zara guide the evolution of the town plan right in front of my eyes, corralling and incorporating inputs from the various experts and using opposition and counter arguments in a healthy, non-confrontational way to steer the design forward and keep it going in the right direction.

"Water storage tanks have to be at the highest point in the town," the water expert chimed in.

"Hospitals have to be readily accessible, so they need to be on main highways, and should be no more than thirty minutes from the furthest ends of the town," the health expert shared his input and Zara added that to the town design which was being projected on the whiteboard in real time.

By the evening, most of the details of the town layout were hammered out and most of the planning concerns had been addressed or incorporated into the design.

"This is very good. We will make some final revisions to the township plan and present it to the mayor early next week. Thank you very much for your collective input." Zara closed the session once there was general consensus and comfort across the room that the town design that they'd developed in that room that day was good.

"I enjoyed being part of your session today. Thank you for inviting me. When you started the session in the morning, did you know that you would have the right layout for the town by the end of the session?" I was awestruck at the ease with which she channelled everyone's input to develop a solution to such a massively complex problem that can impact the lives of all the citizens who would ever live in Dunbar, that was agreeable to the various experts in the room.

"Urban planning and town planning has been an important part of my life right from my childhood. For refugees, proper town planning or makeshift settlement planning can mean the difference between a healthy hygienic life or a life filled with filth and squalor," she said as she was packing up her stuff and getting ready to head out of the atrium.

"After having done this a few times, don't you already know what the right layout is for any town?" I asked, curious to understand how her fascinating brain worked.

"You are partially correct, in that most towns can probably follow the one optimal layout that has worked elsewhere. But each town's geography and topology is unique and the focus of the town and its people could be different. You know, some may want to focus on tourism, others on raising kids and still others on senior citizens. Those variables lead to very different answers in terms of town plan, which in term will make the town unique," she continued as she headed towards the door with me in tow.

"Also there is a second even more important reason for these brainstorming sessions. Involving the experts from the town this early in the design process gets them to invest their time and energy in the final design outcome. With their investment in time and effort, it is their baby and their plan, and because of that they will be committed to implementing their design rather than presenting opposition or creating roadblocks." She understood people. Her ability to work with people and corral the troops towards a common goal reminded me of Samarjit, who instinctively knew how to lead and to build a loyal following. They both were very different personalities, but they both understood people at a fundamental level and that allowed them to inspire others – be it to win glory on the hockey field or build great towns and cities.

As I followed her out of the atrium, I couldn't help but wonder how someone so beautiful and delicate had managed to go through so much as a refugee, as a persecuted minority, and still stay positive in life. Instead of attracting pity for her past, she came across as a beacon of hope and radiated blindingly brilliant optimism, wherever she went.

Despite going through such hardships, here was this highly intelligent woman, who commanded respect from her peers and experts alike, contributing so much to others in this country. Her service to her Yazidi community and to the broader American community was truly remarkable. In her desire and passion to be of service to others, she reminded me of papa.

"Have you been able to pull the contact information of all the Yazidis that are on internet?" Zara asked as she walked up the driveway to my house.

"Yeah, we are almost there. Come on in, Krishna and Rob should be here anytime soon," I replied as I was finishing up my coffee in the patio and headed inside with Zara following me behind.

Over the next few weeks, Zara would come over almost every evening to my house as it became the base of her operations for helping out the Yazidi community. In my own way, I was glad to be of help to the Yazidi community as I knew that is what papa wanted of me, to be spending my life in the service of others and deep in my heart, in my own selfish way, I was glad to see that it also contributed to Zara's happiness.

On days she didn't show up, I would be miserable. I knew then that this was more than just friendship. But I was too self-conscious to ever venture out and make the first move, given my condition. I could engage anyone at the intellectual level, but when it came to the physical aspects, I was never comfortable.

So it came as a relief and pleasant surprise, when during the search for Yazidis on internet, I was able to locate the whereabouts of Iman, Zara's cousin, who she had lost contact with at a very young age. When she found that Iman was well and living in Germany currently, she jumped with joy and hugged me, and in the heat of the excitement kissed me on my lips. At first, it was just a short quick kiss, but soon turned into something deeper and longer, leaving me totally breathless as my heart was pounding away, ready to explode.

"Sorry, I got carried away," she blushed as stepped away. "Thank you for locating Iman. I thought I had lost her."

"No need to be sorry." I didn't know how else to convey what I just felt.

"I have wanted to do that for a while now, but was waiting for you to make the first move," Zara confessed, still blushing.

"I am not good with these things. Given my physical condition, I am never comfortable with these things," I mumbled, despite my best attempts to sound coherent.

"I find you very attractive, and your mind and intelligence to be sexy." She came by and hugged me more passionately this time and kissed me again.

That night she stayed over and it ended up being the most amazing night of my life. For the first time in my life, despite everything else, I felt complete, having her snuggle up next to me in my bed.

It was the beginning of an amazing time in my life. Zara loved travelling, visiting both natural landscapes and also well-planned townships across America. She provided the motivation, and I bought a recreational vehicle which was a big bus with its own bathroom, bedroom, and kitchen that allowed me to travel without having to be dependent on anyone, as it had been fitted with the right equipment and fixtures for me to function quite independently.

Over the next couple of summers, Zara and I would load up the bus and go off on month-long trips to large natural parks and resorts. Along the way, we made stops at Dunbar township to meet the town mayor who was extremely thankful to Zara for her help in the township design and handed her the ceremonial town key for the entire day that we spent in Dunbar.

Despite the many towns and cities covered as part of my travels with Zara, the one city that made an impression on me was Las Vegas. Although when people hear the name Las Vegas, it evokes images of gambling, mafia and everything sinful and amoral. But that is not what I saw when I arrived there. I actually saw a barren desert landscape not that different from Pokhran, with searing hot temperatures that would melt the tires of the cars, barely any clouds in the sky, almost zero humidity, very little natural wild greenery, and no natural sources of water, except for the lake formed by Hoover dam on Colorado river. If Las Vegas can become such a thriving oasis in the midst of Nevada desert, why can't Pokhran be a similar shining oasis in the middle of Thar desert?

"The planning of the business district and Las Vegas strip was excellent," I said as we passed through the city.

"But the rest of the town is not very well designed. The city is good for tourists who visit here, but the town people who stay here face terrible infrastructure and suboptimal facilities. It can be so much better for both tourists and residents if done properly," she continued. Town design was her passion and her eyes would light up when she started discussing it. And I was quite happy to listen to her perspectives and realize that I would see the same town in a totally new light after her analysis.

As we came to the end of our tour of Las Vegas and it started to get dark, we drove towards nearby Grand Canyon with its majestic valleys and canyons and parked ourselves in the RV Park. The spot had a clear view of the entire canyon that stretched out as far as the eye could see. As sun set over the horizon, the sky was filled with orange light and the temperatures cooled down dramatically, and Zara lit the wood logs to make fire and heat up the food. She had pitched a tent on the ground as she wanted to sleep under the open sky next to the camp fire.

"Love the orange light and the shadows in the canyon. Come sit next to me," she tapped on the sleeping bag next to her.

"I love you," she looked into my eyes as she said those words.

"I love you too," my words just flowed. That moment was just perfect. I was completely at peace. All the thoughts of anguish – about going after papa's murderers, rescuing Devyani, losing Samarjit – that used to haunt me and were my constant companions for a long time had suddenly gone quiet, as if they simply vanished from my mind.

Chapter 7
Marrying Zara
(2010)

"Why don't you join my political party? I can get our party to offer an MLA ticket for you in Leh," Subramaniyam spoke to Ranvir, sipping his morning coffee while sitting at the dining table in Ranvir's apartment. Subramaniyam had taken time off from his busy political life to visit his eldest and brightest son to steer him away from his financially unsound and rather unconventional outlook on life and work.

"Thanks for the offer. But I am not interested, dad," he replied knowing fully well that his father would continue to push him to join politics.

"At this point, I am quite happy building artificial glaciers in and around the Ladakh region. I admire Norphel Chewang for all the innovative work he has done in that region, building temporary dams with artificial glaciers and thereby improving water catchment for irrigation there." Ranvir had joined the Jammu & Kashmir rural development authority to work with Norphel, who was also known as the Ice Man for his discovery and use of artificial glaciers.

"That work pays peanuts. Why even bother doing it!" Subramaniyam wanted his son to do well in life and not make stupid mistakes that he would regret later on in life.

"I like building things with my hands. I like seeing real impact of my efforts. My efforts over the past couple of years have provided regular drinking water for people of over fifty villages here. That is worth a lot more to me than any gold and that is what motivates me to get up out of my bed every day," he responded while recognizing that is not how Subramaniyam measured success in life.

"You can have even greater impact by getting involved in politics. While touching many more people's lives, you will also be making a lot more money." Subramaniyam knew, beyond the shadow of a doubt, what was right for his son. In his head it was clear that it was only a matter of time before Ranvir would realize the truth and come around.

"Earning money for the sake of sustenance or just to accumulate wealth doesn't interest me, dad. Especially the underhanded way in which money is currently made in politics in India has zero appeal for me," Ranvir spoke as he walked out onto the balcony of his apartment that was located on the slope of a steep hill. It was a crisp, chilly morning with powdery whiteness all around from the fresh snow that had accumulated on the roof tops all the way down into the valley below.

"You used to work for bare minimum government salary when you were a nuclear scientist, right? Was that so bad?" Ranvir enquired as Subramaniyam walked out of the room to join him, curious to figure out how his dad viewed his time as a scientist for the Indian government.

"Precisely! I loved the scientific complexity and the academic challenge part of it and the nuclear deterrence capability that we managed to build for India. Moreover that was a different time. Right after India got Independence, people across the government were more patriotic, so there was a real desire to help the country even though the pay itself was terrible." Subramaniyam reflected back to those times when he was more of an idealist himself.

"Now everyone in India, or at least those with political power, seem to care only about lining their own pockets rather than doing anything for the progress of the country. With that mindset prevalent among the majority, every man or woman has resorted to fending for themselves without regard for the country as a whole," Subramaniyam continued to speak, and Ranvir could see that there was still a tiny fire of idealism alive in his dad, buried under layers of indifference hardened by years of greed and power struggles that go with becoming a politician in India.

"I don't want to be one of the majority that don't seem to care about others. I don't want to be adding to the problem; I want to be a part of the solution. Moreover, whatever I am doing here, I am pretty darn good at it!" Ranvir never minced words. Although he had the greatest respect for his father, he was not willing to give up what he believed to be right just to appease his father.

"They can't expel you from this college just because of a kiss in public!" Priya was furious and pacing wildly in her hostel room, as Jayanti was packing up her stuff. She had been asked to check out from the hostel and the college campus by the end of that night. Jayanti's face and eyes appeared swollen from crying. Even now, as she went about picking up and arranging her clothes and other things, she couldn't control her tears that were streaming down her cheeks.

It was her final year at St. Stephen's College, Delhi, and she had worked very hard to make sure that her grades were good enough to continue to receive the financial scholarship that would pay for her college fees and her hostel stay as well. Both her parents were school teachers in a village and without that scholarship, it wouldn't have been possible for her to attend any college, leave alone being at St. Stephen's. If she returned to her village near Bhopal, with the news that she was expelled from her college for kissing another girl, then there is no way her parents would have her back and support her lifestyle choice. And even if her parents were to accept her, they would likely find living in that village next to impossible. The stigma would be too great for the villagers to simply ignore.

"All you did was kiss someone that you love. Why should it matter to anyone, that it was another girl who was involved and not a boy." Priya was Jayanti's roommate and a final year student of Economics and Political Science.

Priya Pant was one of the shortest in her class, but she was a dynamite and a bundle of energy that refused to back down from any form of injustice or unfair treatment, whether it was on or off campus. She was one of those girls that don't put too much thought into their dress or makeup, but still manage to look good at all times. Her bright open face, intelligent eyes, and her total disregard for her own self or her ego, revealed a personality that cared more about others than about her personal gain in all matters. Any major policy decisions or demonstrations at the college, she would inevitably get involved in either because she cared about the issue or somebody else would've pulled her in for gaining support for their side of the argument.

Regardless of how she got involved in any policy issue, she always took the side of what she believed to be the right thing to do in that situation. If her friends were on the wrong side of the issue, she would sympathize with them but her support and defence would always be for the right side of the issue.

"Majority does not make it right," she continued her pacing as she spoke, with her gaze locked onto Jayanti.

"You are not leaving the campus tonight. We are going to speak with the college board tomorrow and fight against your expulsion," she started taking Jayanti's clothes out of her suitcase and placing them back into the closet.

"The security guards are supposed to escort me out of the campus by 7 p.m. tonight. How can you stop them?" Jayanti was glad to have

Priya on her side, although she knew that the chances of getting the college board to reverse their decision were zero to none.

"I will call my dad right now. He knows our Dean very well." With that, Priya stepped out to speak with her father, leaving Jayanti behind in the hostel room.

"Papa, I can't believe our college rules! Such illustrious alumni, many members of parliament, most number of Rhodes Scholars of any other college in the country, and still the thinking of the college administration is stuck in the twentieth century," she blurted out as she heard her father's voice at the other end. Although she had a lot of great qualities, patience was not one of them.

"Slow down, slow down! Tell me what happened," Narendra Pant tried to calm her down. He had faced enemy bullets and bombs in battle, led the successful detonation of the "Smiling Buddha" nuclear test and managed to survive through all that because he had learnt to deal with any situation in a calm, level-headed manner. But he hadn't been able to impart that quality to his baby girl.

"The college board has decided to expel Jayanti, my roommate," she replied, trying to get her emotions under control.

"Why?" he asked.

"They decided to expel her on two counts. Firstly, because Jayanti has a relationship with another girl and same sex relationships are not allowed according to the college by laws. Secondly, because she engaged in public display of that relationship, as Jayanti was caught kissing a girl from a different college," she tried to summarize everything that had happened in the past twenty-four hours.

"The college board is made up of old buzzards who are too slow to change. What do you want me to do?" He got right to the point. Although he had attended the same college many years back and the current Dean was his friend, he had no major influence over the rest of the college board.

"I want you to call the Dean and delay Jayanti's expulsion by a week. I want her to be around and on the campus while we fight to get that decision reversed." She had regained her clarity of thought. She had a plan and knew exactly how she was going to go about it.

"OK! I will call him, but can't guarantee how he will react or how much of a say he has in being able to delay the decision. Anything else?" Even though he was retired now and had more time on his hand, he still kept his phone calls crisp and short out of habit from the past.

"Yes, actually. When I sit down with the college board, any advice on how I got about convincing them to reverse the decision?" she asked as she had immense faith in her father's ability to work with and influence people.

"I may be stating the obvious, but here goes nothing. Try to meet with each member of the college board one on one, where it is easy to block out the herd mentality. Start with convincing those that are on the fence and then work your way to the most vocal and staunchest opponents. Most folks tend to go after the most vocal opposition first, but in doing so they end up having very little or no support in the room and will lead to disaster." He was proud of his daughter, especially for the fire she had in her.

"You know, around four thousand BC after the great flood in Mesopotamia, many Yazidis moved east to India and continued to live there till two thousand BC, when some of them returned to their native land to found the historical civilization of Babylonia and Assyria. The rest of the Yazidis continued their absorption into the Hindu culture," Zara's grandfather came and sat next to my wheelchair, transcribing the Kurmanji Kurdish writing on the walls of the Yazidi shrine that was located on the outskirts of Qerebaş village in Syria.

The shrine was a couple of kilometres from the village, with carved stone pillars that were over twenty feet tall, and a stone slab roof which had opened up in some parts allowing shafts of sunlight to stream into the inner sanctum of the temple throughout the day. To the right side of the shrine entrance was carved into stone, the figure of a fully stretched out snake, which stood vertically on its tail, serving as a gatekeeper or a guardian of the shrine. In the centre of the shrine and on the walls were the carvings of Tawsi Melek, the peacock angel, who was sent down to the earth by god to serve as the bearer of both good and the bad.

It was late afternoon, and there was nobody else in the shrine except for Zara's parents, who were also visiting with us from USA, her grandparents, who lived in Qerebaş all their lives, and her immediate family, including uncles, aunts and cousins. The women and the men of the family were dressed in the traditional Yazidi garb – long, colourful dresses, ankle-length pants, embroidered and bedazzled bandanas covering the hair for women, and very loose billowing pants, shirts with loose long sleeves, large fabric belts, and turbans for men.

Zara was dressed in a peach-orange, flowing, dress with white pants that stood out against the green shrubs, and the sand brown backdrop of the shrine. She looked so amazingly lovely that I just couldn't take my eyes off of her. While busy with the activities with her family, every once in a while, her eyes would try to find me, making sure that I was doing well holding on my own with her family and relatives. Although I tried not to think about it too much, especially knowing that she could have anyone she wanted, from time to time I couldn't help myself from wondering as to what she saw in me to be able to want to be with me.

After the prayers, the family gathered around the long table that was set up under the shade of two large mulberry trees, for lunch. The cool breeze from the Mediterranean Sea, the soft rustling of the mulberry leaves above, the chatter of guests around the lunch table, tinkling of the wine glasses, clear blue skies, and the company of Zara – I realized that life probably couldn't get any better than that.

Khurto, Zara's grandfather, loved to talk and he wanted me to know about their family background and about their religion, "According to our religion, Zara won't be able to go to heaven or her soul won't evolve as she is marrying someone outside of our religion. Our belief system dictates that one must marry within the Yazidi community in order to continue the process of evolution of soul, which is expected to happen over multiple lives. She must love you very much to be willing to make such a big sacrifice."

I could detect no hatred or malice in his voice towards me, for taking Zara away from the Yazidi religious beliefs. He was trying to emphasize the fact that his granddaughter was moving mountains and giving up a lot to tie the knot with me.

"Mithra is our central god," he continued while sipping on his wine.

"Is it the same Mithra, the god in the Indian Vedas, for dawn and for ensuring safe traversal of sun through the day?" I asked, surprised at the mention of the Vedic God in Yazidi context.

"Yes, our god was Mithra until about 1100 AD, when Sheikh Adi, our spiritual leader, transformed the Yazidi religion to include elements of Christianity, Judaism and Islam. He changed the narrative at that time and articulated that the very first Yazidi was the son of Adam who was born when god tested the seeds (or beads of sweat) from both Adam and Eve by placing them in separate jars and leaving them to incubate. After nine months, he opened Eve's jar that only had insects and worms, whereas Adam's jar had a beautiful baby. The baby boy grew up and got married, and from him descended all the Yazidi people," Khurto elaborated.

That conversation and the peaceful setting took me way back to my childhood days when didi and I used to hang out with Devyani and her grandfather, Charu Dada, and listen to his stories about Charvakas and their travails and tribulations after India gained Independence from the British.

"Yazidis believe that we have survived seventy-two persecutions so far, and as we don't have recorded history till recently, it is likely that the number is even higher," Khurto responded with a smile, his eyes filled with sadness. He must've been a very handsome man when he was younger. Even now, at over seventy years old, his weather-beaten face, tanned in the Syrian sun, showed a high degree of intelligence and energy.

"Yazidis believe that every living thing has a soul and that the souls are on a journey of purity through the cycle of birth and death. That's why we don't base our life decisions based on just this one life, but also the potential impact of the journey or evolution of our souls. As a result, there is a natural tendency amongst our people to be of peaceful nature, to respect all living things, and to live in harmony with nature. People from others religions, who do not take the time to understand our beliefs, end up thinking of us as devil worshippers and as weak because of our desire to stay non-violent and peace-loving," he paused as Zara came by to serve Knafeh bulbul's nest, a mouth-watering Syrian dessert, to the both of us.

"*Sipas ji were, Zara,*" he spoke in Kurdish, thanking her.

"*Tu bi xêr hatî, bapîrê,*" she responded as she flitted away to help at the other end of the table.

"She has turned out to be such a thoughtful young woman. God bless her life and her soul," he looked at her with admiration and loving care.

"I wish we had a nation of our own where we would never be persecuted in the future. America is the only such nation right now, willing to help us to some extent, but then entry into America is so very hard to gain. The only other nation I can think of, where we could live in peace is India, but India has problems of its own and is not organized enough to provide support for religious refugees like us." He looked on wistfully into the distance as he gulped down the last drop of wine in his glass.

"*Kir ku tu wî bi felsefe, bapîrê,*" Zara spoke smiling at her grandfather, asking him whether he had bored me with his philosophy.

"Thank you for patiently listening to grandpa, my love," she turned towards me as she bent down and kissed me. A sudden calm fell around the shrine as the birds had finally settled down into their nests and their sounds had dropped to rustling of feathers and the leaves, the breeze from the Mediterranean had all but died down, the sky was almost dark with stars popping out of the darkness above, the scattered street lights in the village came online, and I could feel Zara's heartbeat against my chest as she hugged me tight with her intoxicating smell doing wonders on me. Nothing else existed for me in that instance – not the Yazidi struggles, or the Pokhran battles. I did not know before Zara that such peace and contentment was possible.

"When did you know that Zara was the one for you?" Narin asked, looking at me as she came back with a big batch of firewood to add to the open air fire pit. It was a dark starry night with a slight chill in the wind, and the warmth from the dancing fire was just enough to offset the chill. The surrounding air still carried the remnants of the smells from the meats roasted over the fire pits earlier in the night, for the ceremonial dinner.

Zara's cousin Narin, the nineteen-year-old, bright-eyed girl, was attending college in Aleppo. She admired Zara and was following in her footsteps to get out of the village, to attend college and to have a career which was not the traditional path for most Yazidi women, who are expected to take care of home and family as their primary duty.

"The very first time I saw her in the grocery store in Cambridge, I was smitten, and knew that she was the one for me," I replied glancing at Zara, who was reclining in the hammock that was strung between two large oak trees, looking at me with a curious smile, to see what my response would be.

"She is intelligent, dazzlingly beautiful, amazingly graceful, confident, and could have any man she wanted. So the question was never about me being with her and choosing to spend my life with her; it was about why on earth would she ever want to be with me! Even now, despite being here at this juncture and about to be married, I still don't know what she sees in me," I trailed off overwhelmed with emotions at that moment.

"He has done everything he could to push me away – be it his fear that we may not be able to have healthy babies, that I might tire of his physical disabilities, or that he just does not measure up to any of the good-looking guys that would try to ask me out," Zara interjected with a smile, while Narin sat there next to the fire pit adding more firewood to it, fully engrossed in the conversation.

"All those times, even though I was pushing her away and making her think and evaluate the situation logically, I was secretly hoping that she would decide to stick with me," I continued, as Zara slid out of the hammock and came over and hugged me tight as tears rolled down her cheeks.

"You cannot get rid of me that easily. You idiot!" She looked at Narin to say, "Despite his self-deprecating statements and his utter lack of confidence in himself when it comes to women, I find him extremely adorable. He has a compassionate heart, is super smart, with a very rich imagination. He makes me feel beautiful, loved and like I am the only woman in the world for him. When I met him and kissed him for the first time, I felt complete. There was no more desire to go anywhere or seek any further, I was content. That is when I knew he was the one for me." Zara picked up where I left off.

There was a long pause as all three of us were lost in our thoughts as if in a trance with our eyes and our collective gaze fixed on the fire.

"Yazidis are not allowed to marry outside of our religion. How did you make that transition in your mind?" Narin asked Zara.

Zara told me much later that Narin was curious about the issue of marrying outside of the religion as she was in love with a Christian senior from her college.

"I guess when you find the one that you are meant to be with, everything else just settles in your mind. At least for me that was and still is the case. There has been no conflict with god or religion in my head, because I know that our god will understand. I am happy when I am with Chaitanya and miserable when I am away from him. I can't imagine any god that would want me to be miserable." That was the first time I had heard Zara articulate her religious views as it pertained to our relationship together.

The flames flickered on, while the roasted meat smell was all but gone, replaced by the smell of myrrh and lavender that Narin was adding to the fire along with a fresh batch of firewood. The new moon was all the way overhead and was clearly visible jutting out of the dark mountains over the horizon.

"How and when did you propose to Zara?" Narin asked looking at me, after another long pause.

"It took me a while to gather enough courage to ask her to marry me. It was three years after we first met, before I decided to propose to her. The delay was not because I was not sure at my end, rather it was because I was not sure whether she would ever want me," I started trying to answer her question.

"I've lost track of the innumerable hints that I'd dropped for him to get comfortable with the idea that I really meant to be with him," Zara added.

"It was my birthday that day and it was late in the night when I returned from my trip to Dunbar, where I had submitted the final township designs to the planning council. Rob and Krishna were at home along with Chaitanya, working on their stuff, as they usually do on most weekdays," she continued.

"As I came into the house, the three of them burst into a 'happy birthday' song, which totally caught me by surprise. They had a bouquet of lovely red roses on the dining table next to the cake. As Krishna lit the candles on the cake, Chaitanya asked me to grab the knife which is when things got interesting," there was excitement in Zara's voice.

"As I opened the drawer to get the knife, I noticed a nicely wrapped gift box, about an inch wide and about the length of a regular pen in the drawer. That caught me by total surprise. I had never had anyone surprise me with a gift placed like that before," Zara choked up as she recounted that day's events. "It was a beautiful diamond bracelet. I wore that bracelet on and proceeded to cut the cake. In order to serve the cake, I opened the kitchen cabinet to pick up some plates. And right there on top of the stack of plates was another gift box wrapped in gold and red paper."

"That box had a lovely necklace with a diamond pendant. My heart was racing now. I opened and checked the remaining cabinets and drawers for any other hidden gifts, while Chaitanya, Rob and Krishna kept smiling all along," Zara went on.

"'Are there any more gifts?' I demanded of Chaitanya, as I couldn't take the suspense anymore."

"Were there any other gifts?" Narin asked, not able to control the suspense herself.

"No. That was the last of it, or at least that is what I thought, till all the four of us sat down to have dinner at the table," Zara continued.

"Around that time I suggested that we should have some wine to celebrate her birthday, knowing fully well that she would head to the wine cellar to pick up a bottle," I chimed in with a grin.

"And as I opened the wine cellar, right there in the middle of it was the same unmistakeable gold and red coloured gift box. Going by the size and shape of the box, my heart skipped a beat. I picked it up and turned around, and right there on the ground was Chaitanya, while Rob and Krishna were right behind him," Zara relayed the moment so well.

"'Will you marry me?' I asked while Rob and Krishna started the chorus 'say yes!'" I filled in for the finish.

Following the rituals of the Yazidi traditional marriage ceremony, after being away for three long days in a dark room, Zara finally showed up at my doorstep accompanied by Nadia, Narin and a couple of other female relatives. As I wheeled up to the door and opened it, they nudged her to move forward while they continued to smile and giggle behind her. Prior to Zara's arrival, I was given a small pebble that I threw gently at her so as to smack her on her shoulder, indicating her submission to me from now and forever. All this submission of women stuff was too much for me, as the equality of men and women was never a question in my mind, but I was fine to go along with the rituals to maintain tradition and to satisfy the wishes of Zara's parents and grandparents.

After throwing the pebble, I turned around and rolled back to the bed and got myself onto it, waiting breathlessly for Zara to join me. She gently closed the bedroom door behind her, shooing away her nosy cousins who were trying to sneak in with their cell phones to take our pictures. She was wearing a lavender coloured flowing silk dress, lime green top and long skirt, long golden ear pieces with purple amethyst stones, a thin short necklace with a single round diamond pendant resting right below the throat at the collarbone, a fine emerald encrusted pendant on her forehead that made her eyes and face light up in the dimly lit room, and a unique ring on her left index finger that appeared to be multiple gold rings with light green emerald stones joined together stretching it from the base of the finger to the first digit. Her shoulder-length hair encased and framed her pretty face in rollicking waves.

Given her otherwise simple yet classy taste in dresses and accessories, the traditional dress and the heavy jewellery was a bit much for Zara. But she wanted to make sure she did not break any other Yazidi traditions, having already broken a central one by marrying me.

She started walking towards me, and I remember thinking, "She looks so fabulously sexy".

"Do you want me to turn off the lights altogether?" she asked stopping about ten feet from the bed.

"You can dim those a bit more, leaving some light on so that I can see your face and your eyes. I would like my mind to make a note of every single visual, sound, smell and sensation from this evening to be replayed when I am old and this youthful time is a distant memory. This will be my happy place to go to, to recharge and to find a reason for living," I rambled on as I got carried away in the moment.

"Aren't you overdoing it a tad bit much?" she smilingly said as she turned towards the light switch.

"Stop right there and take off your dress," I tried to order her in as authoritative a voice as I could muster, just as she was walking up to the bed.

When Zara stood there in that lavender dress on that white marble floor against that lush dark backdrop of the room, it appeared as though she was floating in the air. Frankincense and jasmine scents filled the room, creating an ambience that heightened all senses, especially the sense of touch. Maybe it was the jasmine, but I could feel every part of my body as I lay on the bed, the back of my head resting on the soft pillow, my back resting on the mattress feeling every bump and contour in it, and my exposed limbs sensing the slightest breeze or movement of the curtains. From the backyard, there was a distinctly Arabic music wafting in, composed of oud and qanun sounds that transformed the room into a desert oasis under a dark starry sky.

She stood there very vulnerable and very conscious of herself as she didn't realize how desirable and sexy she appeared, as she took off her lavender overall, lime green top and skirt.

"Come, lie down next to me!" I ordered half jokingly as I slowly started getting used to playing the role of a domineering Yazidi husband, which I knew would be short-lived. Zara let me indulge in that role all the while we were visiting her ancestral village in Syria. And I intended to make the most of it while it lasted.

For the first time in my life, my perception of the passage of time was completely skewed that night. Yazidis have a saying that goes something like time is relative and *"if you spend five hours with a beautiful girl, it feels like it has been only five minutes"*. For me the entire night was both very short and very long, at the same time. Short because it did seem to dissolve into the next day very fast, long because my mind got filled with so many memories that I could replay them over and over again and each time I seemed to focus on some new aspect of the scene that I hadn't noticed before. Whether I perceived it as short or long, in either case it was undeniable ecstasy and joy that was associated with every moment of that entire night.

She was lying on the bed next to me, with her head resting on the white sheets I couldn't help noticing the contrast of her dark hair against the white linen sheets, her beaming eyes, her bewitching smile, and the way she closed her eyes when I gently let out my breath near her ears and kissed the back of her ears. Every touch, every kiss, every caress evoked some pleasant response in her while she moved to my touch as her whole body arched in response.

That lasted way late into the night. The music had died out and everybody had gone off to sleep. I had fallen off to sleep only to wake up to see her snuggling up to me. I was drifting in and out of consciousness as there was such an overload of emotion, sensations and holistic experiences. I never thought I was capable of making her physically happy, but then she adapted and my body learnt to respond, and as a result, I got to test my own limits and to make my body do more than what I thought possible.

As she reached her climax, it was sheer delight to watch her whole body writhe and contort in an orgasmic seizure, leaving her totally drained and gasping for breath. Her scent filled my nostrils and enveloped my brain, while the taste of her sweat left me wanting for more.

Chapter 8
Zara Visits Syria
(2010-2015)

"I am feeling ecstatic today!!" Zara chirped with excitement over the Skype video call from her hotel room in Aleppo.

"For the first time, I could feel the baby kicking today. It was such a soft movement, felt like butterflies in my stomach," she continued. Despite her hectic schedule in Cambridge, she decided to travel to Syria to visit her grandparents and extended family as part of her family tradition. Before heading out to Karabash, she was spending a couple of days in Aleppo to do some shopping and to speak about her work and her career at Narin's college.

"Is Narin staying with you at your hotel?" I asked, recognizing that in her current state she might need assistance and also a local guide to help navigate the streets of old Aleppo city.

"Don't worry, I am well taken care of here. Yes, she is with me, and she just went downstairs to pick up dinner," she responded with a smile, addressing the concern in my voice, as she settled in the large, king-size bed with an antique headrest studded with colourful glass work and bold calligraphy on the wall behind the headrest.

"Quite a few of Narin's friends attended my talk on urban planning and architecture at her college. Most of them came by afterwards with questions about my life in the States, about succeeding in my chosen career as a woman, and about emigrating to more tolerant countries in North America or Europe," she continued recounting her day's events, with me listening on quietly, as she was used to doing it every day in the evening after we got back home.

"Those questions just reinforced what a blessed and privileged life we have in the US. If one were to discount the occasional racist remark or the glare on the street, the life in US is pretty close to as good as it can get," she continued on the topic that was always of interest for her and it reminded me of how I had met her for the first time in that grocery store.

"Hmm…" I thoroughly enjoyed listening to her incisive analysis on culture and policy related topics. Although I agreed with her perspective on US being close to the ideal state, at the back of my mind there was this ever present feeling, during these discussions with Zara, that India gets pretty close to offering similar freedom and rights to its citizens, without the overt and at times violent racial discrimination of the US, albeit with a weaker law enforcement and poorly developed public infrastructure in cities and towns.

"The only thing broken in the US system is that the economic inequality between the rich and the poor is never addressed. It only keeps growing with each generation." That really bothered her, especially with her focus on inner city planning and bringing vitality and levelling the playing field for the underprivileged kids.

"Aren't you supposed to be relaxing and enjoying your time there, so that the baby has a stress-free time?" I smiled, trying to steer her towards a lighter conversation.

"What do you think of the name Pokhran for our baby?" she announced, which caught me by total surprise.

"What if we have a girl?" I asked, still trying to get my mind around the thought of naming the baby.

"Pokhran will go well with our baby girl as well," she declared without hesitation.

"Of all the names in the world, why Pokhran? Are you sure? Especially when that name and place is so intricately tied to the nuclear test and everything in my life that ensued as a result of that." Pokhran was a big part of me. I just never thought of it as a positive association in my life.

"When I first arrived in Pokhran and visited Radhika and her family, I felt like I belonged there. I was unconditionally accepted and felt loved for who I am, which was the first time I ever experienced something like that in my life," she responded.

"People in Pokhran are happy, content and peaceful, even though nothing is really going in their favour – neither the land, the rain, nor the political leaders. But nothing seems to dampen their spirit. I want that eternal hope and optimism to always be with our baby as he or she grows up." There was genuine calm in her voice and she exuded joy and happiness as she reflected on her time in Pokhran.

"And most importantly, the integral role that place has played in your life and in bringing you to me," she replied as tears started rolling down her cheeks. With her pregnancy, these days she seemed to get emotional quite readily, without any significant cause, than she would ever allow herself to at any other time before.

"I love you, my dear," she looked straight into the camera and at me as she mouthed those words slowly and with emphasis. If only I knew how precious those words were and how our happy little world was about to change drastically, I would've just tried to hold on to that moment longer and tried to make it last an eternity.

BLAM!! BLAM!!

There was loud banging on the doors. Startled, Zara looked up from the bed as the doors of her hotel room sprang open and Narin burst into the room. Zara dropped the laptop on the bed, with me still connected to her on the Skype video call.

"We have to leave the hotel room now! The rioters are coming," Narin declared in a frenzy, as she seemed frazzled, blood on her t-shirt, and completely out of breath.

"No time to grab anything else, we have to go now. They just sliced a man in half right there in public on the street, and it happened so close to where I was standing that his blood spilled on me as well. We have to go now," Narin started to head out the door, grabbing Zara's hand and dragging Zara along with her.

It all happened very fast, in probably a few seconds, but those were the longest few seconds of my life. Even before I could say anything, I could see Zara heading out of the hotel room through the same doors that Narin had just burst through. I caught one glimpse of her as she turned around to say what seemed like a goodbye, and for the first time I saw fear in her eyes. She wasn't afraid for her own safety; her fear was for the baby. And then they both were gone.

I sat there looking at my computer and the Skype screen, which just a few moments back was connected to Zara buzzing with lively banter from her time in Aleppo. A million thoughts ran through my head, but nothing seemed to make any sense. Staring at the hotel room wall through the laptop, I couldn't help but think of Pokhran, and Zara with me.

"You are going to have a lovely marriage ceremony in India, and Ramesh and I will be taking care of organizing it." Didi was adamant about conducting an Indian-style marriage ceremony and reception in Pokhran, sort of a second ceremony in addition to the Yazidi-style marriage ceremony in Karabash. Didi knew that it was safe for me to visit India, as the political leadership had changed and most of the old leaders and goons from papa's time, had retired or were no longer in power.

"Zara and you just have to show up here, and the rest you have to leave to me," was a non-negotiable order from didi.

It was the winter of 2012 when Zara and I landed at the Delhi airport. Didi and Ramesh had come by to pick us up and drive us to Pokhran. Zara was ecstatic about visiting India, as this was her first time there, and the first meeting with didi and the rest of the family and friends in person.

"I am so glad you decided to visit us and have your Indian-style marriage ceremony in Pokhran.
Welcome to India and to our family, Zara!" Didi came and hugged Zara as we stepped out of the airport.

"We are delighted to have you here, Zara." Usually reserved, Ramesh voiced with unbridled enthusiasm, clearly glad to see us. It had taken me quite a few years, after didi got married to

Ramesh, that I finally stopped referring to him as 'Ramesh sir'".

"You should catch some sleep on our drive back and rest tonight, because you will be spending the next three days with me away from Chaitu, actually you won't see him till he shows up at the marriage mandap on his white horse on the day of the marriage ceremony," Didi spoke, looking at Zara as we settled into the car on our way to Pokhran.

We felt the cool, winter night breeze as we sped on our way to Pokhran, saw the occasional dhaba with its strictly vegetarian fare as we crossed the state lines into Rajasthan, and the gradual shift of landscape from lush vegetation in Delhi to barren land dotted with shrubs as we drove past Jaipur towards my childhood backyard and my playground. With the jetlag kicking into high gear, I couldn't keep my eyelids open anymore, and surrounded by Zara, didi, and Ramesh, the last thought that I remember before sliding into deep slumber was "It feels good to be home".

Next day, before daybreak, Radhika woke Zara up and took her away to get started on the busy day that she had planned for Zara.

"Come with me, Zara. We will get you showered with turmeric, sandalwood, and these other aromatic herbs that will cleanse your skin and add a new shine to it, while lifting your mood and sense of well being. These other girls from the town have come to meet you and help you with getting prepared and ready over the next three days," Radhika chirped as she introduced Zara to the girls that had joined her in the festivities. The whole town was invited and joined in the celebrations.

"You are making me feel like a princess, Radhika. Thank you for doing all this," Zara was overwhelmed with all the attention, the wonderful smells, and all the helpful people around who took real joy in her marriage to Chaitanya.

"We haven't even scratched the surface of it yet. Right after your shower and your breakfast, we head to Jaipur where we are going shopping for a gold embroidered sari, bangles and accessories that you will wear on the marriage day," Radhika laid out their shopping plan for the day.

"Can you please arrange some breakfast for Chaitu when he wakes up?" Radhika requested Ramesh.

"You know, I haven't seen Chaitu this happy in a long time," Radhika voiced, as Zara and she were on their way to Jaipur.

"How was Chaitanya as a kid?" Zara asked brimming with curiosity, as they both navigated their way through Johari Bazaar, packed with shoppers, street-side food vendors and rows of jewellery shops on both sides of the street. Despite the winter time, it was hot even in the early afternoon, especially surrounded by the hustle and bustle of the bazaar and the heat from the food being prepared right by the street-side. The appetizing sweet and savoury smells from the street-side cooking mixed with the scents of the incense sticks from the surrounding stores and the aroma of the flowers added to the overwhelming sensory richness of the bazaar ambience.

"*Khamma ghani, deviji. Krupaya andar aaiye*," the owner of one of the largest meenakari jewellery stores in the bazaar, came out to greet both of them as he recognized Radhika and invited them into his shop.

As they made their way into Manish's shop, "Our mom, Rajashree, was a fiercely independent and very kind-hearted soul. At a time when families didn't encourage women to attend school, she overcame a lot of resistance inside and outside her house to not only complete her education, but also to start teaching at school. She was intently focused on helping other girls and women in the village to get an education and gain financial independence. Chaitanya never got to feel that love, that I've had the privilege of experiencing, as she died at childbirth," Radhika continued to share details of Chaitanya's childhood. Despite her best efforts to keep the conversation light, she could not stop her tears as she reflected on her time with her mom.

"Whether in his classes or at work, even though his focus is on highly technical subjects, he does not harbour any unequal treatment towards women. I can see that he genuinely believes that whatever men can do, women can do as well. Based on what you just said, it looks like he has got that from his mom," Zara filled in, as she could see the same tendency of Rajashree's manifesting in Chaitanya's perspectives as well.

"Our papa was a more hard-headed, tough as nails and stoic personality. It was very hard to understand what was going on in his head. Until much later in his life, I used to think he was unnecessarily tough on Chaitanya. Only later did I realize that whatever he was doing was to train Chaitu to become a tough adult who could fight the hard battles in life and still persist and win, and not give up at the first sign of resistance. Wish he had shown more of his loving side along with his tough persona, as that would've probably meant a more pleasant childhood for Chaitu than what he got," Radhika continued the reflection on Chaitu's childhood as the storekeepers started placing bangles on display for Zara and helping her try those on.

Zara was enthralled to get this amazing glimpse into the times from Chaitanya's life, before she had met him. "Early on, Chaitu used to be very shy and was picked on by some of the mean boys in his class. But then he met Samarjit, who was the son of a dacoit, an Indian equivalent of Robin Hood. Having Samarjit in his life transformed him from a shy kid to a happier, more vocal boy." Radhika continued, as they paid for the bangles in Manish's shop and stepped out to make their way to one of the biggest sari stores in Johari bazaar.

"Samarjit's parents and Babloo, who is also a dacoit and a friend of both Samarjit and Chaitu, will be arriving here for the marriage ceremony. You will be able to meet them," Radhika continued.

"What happened to Samarjit?" Zara asked, as Chaitanya hadn't spoken much to her about his childhood.

"Samarjit died of a gunshot wound, when the police ambushed their hiding place," Radhika spoke as she sifted through the saris that were placed in front of them.

"Did you meet Devyani?" Zara asked, gingerly trying to hide a tinge of jealousy that surprised even herself, as she didn't realize that she had the capacity to be jealous.

A smile broke out on Radhika's face as she remembered Devyani and their childhood summers spent in Payradanga.

"Chaitu mentioned Devyani to you?" Radhika asked, trying to figure out what could be said or best left unsaid. She knew that her brother could never hide things intentionally; he just might not share as much, of his own accord.

"Just that Devyani was his first crush and his first love," Zara laid it out openly.

"Devyani was a naughty devil. She brought out the prankster in Chaitanya. Both of them would scheme and plot over days on end on how to prank the kids and adults alike in the neighbourhood. She taught him how to swim, among other things. In ways similar to you, she was totally oblivious and blind to Chaitu's physical disabilities. She accepted him as he was," Radhika spoke with a spark in her voice as it brought back memories from happier childhood times.

"When she was kidnapped and taken away from us, it broke all our hearts. More so for Chaitu. He decided to never give up on finding her and bringing her back home. He did manage to find her, but things had changed for Devyani. She has kids now and has decided to make a life with her kidnapper. It broke him but at the same time strengthened his resolve to create a society where women can feel safe and respected, diversity is revered, not just accepted, and all religions are accorded equal rights," Radhika concluded as she pointed to a red sari with white gold embroidery work, for Zara to try on.

"Chaitanya and I discuss and debate such things a lot. Religious tolerance is a topic that is close to my heart, especially given the recent persecution of Yazidis by the various terrorist groups," Zara paused as she took in the entirety of what had happened to Devyani at such a young age. Her heart reached out for that young girl barely in her pre-teens when she was kidnapped. Mostly because she and her family did not have any support from other religious communities around them.

The store owner picked up the red sari and draped it on his arm to show the full length of it.

"That is a beautiful sari!" both Zara and Radhika chimed in unison. Radhika got the sari wrapped and paid for it and both of them stepped back into the evening sun and slightly cooler bazaar where the crowds had changed from shoppers and tourists to local families with kids coming out for the food at the street vendors.

"We should head back to Pokhran now. It is mehendi night today and your palms, arms and feet will be decorated with henna. One of my closest friends is coming over to do the designs. She is very creative and a well regarded artist. Hope you will like her designs," Radhika detailed out the ceremonies and plans for that night as they made their way back to Pokhran.

"Thank for taking me shopping and for sharing Chaitanya's childhood stories." Zara hugged Radhika, overcome with emotion.

"We are a family now. Think nothing of it. Thank you for bringing smiles and happiness back in Chaitu's life."

As homage to papa, didi wanted the wedding *mandap* and the marriage ceremony to be held not in the temple or at a traditional marriage hall, but rather near the canal that papa had designed and built as his life's work. The immediate neighbours and almost the entire town had decided to help out and join in the festivities, setting up coloured twinkling lights along almost half a kilometre stretch of the canal which served as a canopy over the cool fresh water flowing through it. As the sun set in the evening, the decorative lights came on, filling the twilight desert horizon with a magical aura broken only by the silhouette of the occasional khejri tree in the background. The cool winter air was rich with the smells of the foods that the cooks had started preparing in the makeshift kitchen.

"Babloo, can you pick up Chaitu's friends, Rob and Krishna from the Jaipur airport? Their flight was delayed, but should've landed by now," Ramesh asked. Ramesh coordinated all the activities at the ceremony and Babloo was there to pick up any slack, while didi was busy with getting Zara dressed in the red sari with all the trimming, including the *nath*, the big nose ring, the bangles along the full length of both the arms and the traditional pallu over the head and covering the face of the bride.

"I will accompany you on your horse ride to the mandap," Babloo declared, as he offered to get me buckled in for his ride to the ceremony.

"Bring the *paalki* to the house now !" Radhika shouted to get the palanquin over to the door, so that Zara could be carried to the mandap.

Zara looked fabulous in that red sari with the nose ring and the pallu draped over her face, as I made my way up to the mandap on the horse, with Babloo to my side, holding me in place. I had given in to all this extravagance as I knew it would make didi happy and add to the happiness of the town people. I was glad we decided to have this wedding ceremony in Pokhran especially by the side of the canal. I suddenly felt close to papa, through the proximity to the canal, in a way that I'd never felt before. It was a sort of closure for me and a sense of peace dawned on me that made me let go of the terrible circumstances that had led to papa's death, knowing that he has moved on to a different and happier place, and that he would want me to move forward, building a better future for myself and for others around me.

Following some of the rituals and mantras chanted on the mandap, the priest signalled us to make seven circumambulations around the *havan* fire, after tying the knot between Zara's sari and the scarf that was draped around my neck. As both of us started going around the havan, all the guests, including the kids who were till then running around, got on their feet and showered us with rose petals and rice, in a gesture that conveyed their good wishes and blessings to us.

There we were, married a second time, following the Indian or Rajasthani style marriage ceremony!!

"For our second honeymoon, we are spending the night in the middle of the desert in a tent. I've already discussed the preparations with Radhika," Zara indicated as we were escorted out of the mandap, amidst applause and wishes from the assembled guests.

Although I had grown up in this place, I had never slept in the middle of the desert before this. It is probably the curse of familiarity that it takes someone from outside to open up our eyes to things that are unique and interesting in our lives did. Zara looked at Pokhran and the desert so much more differently than any of us who had lived there most of our lives did. She found magic and adventure in traversing the desert, sleeping under the dark starry skies, shopping in the hot dusty bazaars of the place and even looking at the layout and the plan of the town.

"I thoroughly enjoyed spending time with your family and getting to know Pokhran," Zara spoke as she snuggled up to me in the tent which was pitched miles away from the town and from any habitation. It was just the two of us, the desert, the crisp, chilly air, the clear, cloudless, night sky and total, absolute silence.

"Radhika is just absolutely amazing and she loves you so much. You are truly blessed to have such a caring, loving sister," she continued.

"She took care of me since when I was a baby. She is my only family and I just can't imagine making it through life this far without her being around," I trailed off thinking of all the times in my life when she had picked me up and pushed me to keep moving.

"This place has so much diversity in terms of looks, languages, lifestyles, and religious beliefs, but nobody seems to be putting down anybody else, nobody is discriminating against anybody else, and more importantly, nobody is constantly stereotyping others just because they are different from the rest. Here, diversity is accepted if not celebrated, which is a better way of living than in Europe or in US where diversity seems to be tolerated at best," Zara slid into the topic that was close to her heart.

"Too heavy a topic for us to discuss tonight, honey. Don't you think?" I smiled as I tried to steer her away onto more fun and lighter topics.

"Hahaha..." she laughed as she traced her fingers along my lips.

"I have a point to make here, and then I will shut up," she continued with a smile, not willing to give up the thought just yet. "Over the past few days I have got to know this place and the people quite well. You know, I believe that Pokhran has the potential to be India's Las Vegas and maybe even much more than that. It can also be a beacon of a lifestyle and culture where diversity is celebrated and serve as a statement that India can send out to the rest of the world that it has arrived on the world stage, not just by selfishly focusing on its own needs but extending its hospitality and magnanimous heart to help those in need, such as embracing world refugees and providing an asylum for those who are persecuted elsewhere. It has already done this silently over the ages, but it can do so more formally and broadcast it to the rest of the world," Zara continued, unable to contain the emotion and the passion that she felt for Pokhran and everything surrounding it.

"Maybe. Although I am not certain whether as a nation and a population, India has the capacity to ever present such an organized front to everybody else in the world. Everything in India evolves and comes into existence organically without any planned action." I realized that, without meaning to, I was dampening her optimism and her appreciation of the country and its people.

"If only you could see it with my eyes. As an outsider, I can see that despite the chaos, there is stability and peace in this place. More importantly, people here are happy and content. In another life and maybe in an alternate universe, India would be the perfect place where the Yazidis could coexist peacefully with the rest of the religions and may even thrive." Her eyes were looking at things way beyond the stars, as she spoke, knowing that such easy solutions don't readily show up in this universe. At least not in our lifetime.

Time flies when you are having fun and seems to be zooming past way too quickly when things are mostly going our way.

It was about three years since our marriage, early 2015, when Rob and Krishna burst into my office with broad beaming smiles.

"We got great news for you!" Krishna let out, unable to curb his enthusiasm.

Right about the same time, Zara decided to pop into my office. Just one of those days when she was able to take off from her busy work schedule and make time to join me for lunch.

"I picked up some sandwiches on my way over here. Good to see you both," she said looking at Rob and Krishna in my office.

"Perfect timing, Zara! We have excellent news to share with you all," Krishna chimed in.

"Oh wow. This is going to be a fantastic lunch then. I have good news to share as well afterwards," Zara added, while waiting for Krishna to go on with his news first.

Rob and Krishna had been working with translating the social media mining software that we'd been developing over the past few years into a software company. It was my hobby as well as a way for me to stay engaged with my friends and the industry while teaching in the classroom. I had a pretty good idea that the news from Krishna and Rob must have something to do with that company. I was more curious about the news that Zara wanted to share.

"Some of the biggest companies in the social media and marketing research space have been reaching out to us, as you already know, with the intent of acquiring our algorithms and software for significant sums of money. Today we received the best offer from the largest marketing research and polling company in the world," Krishna continued with his usual hyperbole and inclination for the dramatics.

"They offered us a lot of money. You ready to hear this?" He paused with a beaming smile, looking at each of us around the room.

"Come on, Krishna! I am dying with suspense here. Spill the beans fast," Zara rushed him along.

"We got offered five hundred million dollars for our company. That would mean both Rob and I make about a hundred million each, while Chaitanya pockets a cool two hundred and fifty million. Each of our research associates, that are still students at the college, will walk away millionaires as well!" he finally came out with the news.

I didn't need any more money. I had everything that I ever wanted. Seeing Rob and Krishna happy and making the lives of our research associates better made that offer very fulfilling. After the basic needs are met, any additional wealth does not bring incremental joy by itself. For me, the joy was in deploying that capital towards paying back to the town that had given me so much.

"Congratulations to the three of you. You guys deserve it for all your genius and the hard work you put into it," Zara came over and hugged me tightly.

"Now your turn, honey. What was the news you wanted to share?" I was scanning Zara to pick up any hints of what the news could be. Maybe it was approval for the urban planning research grant that she was pushing for over the past six months.

"I am pregnant. We are going to be parents!" Zara jumped with joy and looked into my eyes waiting for my response.

I was happy beyond belief and at a total loss for words. This was indubitably the best day of my life, while also being the scariest because I knew at the bottom of my heart that I wasn't meant to have a good time in my life. Things were not supposed to be going so well for me, and whenever they did, it just meant a terrible time was lurking right around the corner, waiting to pounce on me anytime.

My mind was racing frantically, trying to figure all options to get to know the whereabouts of Zara and Narin. The news on the TV was filled with the chaos and mayhem across Syria as the riots spread out from Aleppo to across the entire country. All the phone lines into the country were jammed as the rioters attacked the communication infrastructure.

Running out of time and out of options, I reached out to John Ratcliffe, the private investigator, who had become somewhat of a friend and stayed in touch long after he had helped me with locating and connecting with Devyani.

"John, I need your help," I spoke with a trembling voice.

"What's up?" John was not one for pleasantries and neither would he let any emotions cloud his interactions or his judgement. Although he must've noticed my trembling voice, he didn't show any sign of recognizing it or calling special attention to it.

I filled him in on the events leading up to the Skype call when Narin had burst into the hotel room and rushed Zara out with her.

"Where was she staying?" John asked, as he got into his private investigator mode.

"She was at Mansouriya Hotel, in the old city of Aleppo," I could barely focus my mind as I mouthed off those words.

"Send me latest pictures of both Zara and Narin. I have a couple of operatives in Syria. I will get in touch with them right away. Give me twenty-four hours and I will get back to you with Zara's whereabouts. In case my operatives can't find them, I will fly into Istanbul myself and cross over into Syria. We will get them back, Chaitanya." That was the first time I sensed a hit of emotion in John's voice.

All of a sudden, John's words brought comfort at a time when nothing could've ever helped. At that moment, he was my god, my float in a stormy sea with troubled waters.

It seemed like an eternity as I waited for John to get back to me with information about Zara.

Chapter 9
Ends Justify the Means
(2015-2019)

"I can't breathe... somebody, please help!" She started clawing and grasping at anything in the darkness that could get her out of what seemed like a plastic body bag that she found herself in, as she regained consciousness.

She heard a faint shuffling in the distance, which made her stop the struggling as she waited intently to hear what the sound was and where it was coming from. At first it felt like a single set of steps that started to approach her, and pretty soon they were joined by what seemed like three or four more pairs of steps. She could feel those feet circle around her, as a hand reached down to her body bag and started fiddling with the zipper.

"Who are you? Please don't hurt me!" Her voice was close to a shriek as she tried to plead with her assailants, while her mind tried to piece together as to how she ended up in this body bag. The last memory she had was attending a job interview for an e-commerce company in Jaipur. She had flown in from Delhi specifically for that interview.

Her mind was racing as she was slowly coming about. Could it have been a long time since she was knocked out unconscious?

How many days had she been in that body bag?

"Relax! Don't struggle and stay still for a bit, and we will help you out of the body bag." It was a soothing but firm male voice. Although the voice was calming and seemed friendly, she just could not get herself to trust anyone.

"Give me a hand with the zipper, John!" the same soothing voice continued.

Finally, there was a name for her mind to latch on to, as her scared mind tried to make sense of whatever was happening around her and to her.

Finally, after a bit of struggle, the zipper of the body bag opened slowly, flooding her eyes with the surrounding bright white light as her iris constricted trying to adjust to the blinding light. It almost seemed like daylight, until she noticed that there were no windows anywhere on those pure white walls, covered with a white roof and white tiled floor. It was a huge room or rather a very large warehouse about the size of a football field, stretching hundreds of feet on both sides.

As her eyes got adjusted to the brightness, she could focus on the faces surrounding her. She looked around as she could make out five faces. She was almost expecting them to be all men, and was caught off guard when she spotted a female face among them. In a way, her mind was preparing for the worst case scenario, and finding a female face amongst her assailants gave her some sense of hope. She was a realist and had assessed her current situation as something beyond hope, whether there was a female assailant in the mix or not.

Once her feet were out of the body bag, she tried to get up, but her feet would not budge an inch. She felt paralyzed.

"You won't be able to get up just yet. The drug has to fully wear off before you can move your limbs," the same soothing voice spoke. She saw a tall man in his early thirties, with an athletic build, and with a light stubble. For a kidnapper and a bad guy, he appeared to have a very friendly open face and his eyes conveyed kindness and comfort without a single word being said.

"I am Ranvir. Thank god that you finally came about. We were all getting concerned about you," he extended his hand.

"You kidnap me, drug me and bring me here and expect me to become friends with you!" she tried to express her anger as she gathered her bearings.

"What!" Ranvir and the others seemed surprised, "You think we kidnapped you?"

"Yes!"

"Ha ha," Ranvir let out a gentle knowing laugh while the others smiled. "No, we are not laughing at you, rather at the irony of the situation. It is just that we were brought here in precisely the same manner as you have been brought here as well. We realize you are just regaining consciousness and will need some time to acclimatize to your new surroundings. Allow us to prop you up against the wall so that you can eat something and regain some strength."

Her mind continued to race, trying to make sense of this new information and for the first time since she regained consciousness, she was less scared and more confused.

Before she could say anything, Ranvir and the woman caught hold of both her arms, each on either side of her and picked up her limp body and propped it against the wall. Now that she could focus and see normally, she realized that the room was even larger than she earlier thought it to be and also the ceiling was higher than usual. She felt like she was in a rectangular cathedral with very smooth, white walls, white floor, and white ceiling, and not a single pillar or support to obstruct the view of the entire room in any direction. Although the room was flooded with light, as if it were daylight, not a single lighting fixture was visible, hidden away from sight, giving it the feel of natural sunlight. Without a single window to break the smooth monotony of the white walls, her mind concluded that it must be all artificial light around her. So she couldn't really tell whether it was night or day.

As her eyes wandered around the whole space, they landed on the dark blue body bag that she had come out of. Right next to her body bag on the floor, she noticed that there were five other body bags. "Maybe they are telling the truth after all," she wondered as she regained her composure enough to make eye contact with Ranvir and the others in the room.

"I am Priya," she finally said sheepishly, as she extended her arm towards Ranvir, embarrassed at herself for suspecting them. Ranvir gave her a warm smile. She was amazed that he was able to maintain his cool so well and comfort others around him, even in such a situation.

"They must've given a bit too much of the drug to you, as you were out almost seven or eight hours longer than the rest of us," Ranvir spoke as the others looked on.

"How long have you guys been here?" Priya spoke, trying to assess the situation while her most recent memories slowly started flooding back into her mind.

"Can't say for sure. There are no clocks in this room, but we don't believe we've been here for more than twenty-four hours," the only other woman in the room spoke, trying to sound calm.

"I am Nagashree." She shook Priya's hand.

At that point, the remaining three in the room – John, Sanjeev and Ahmed – introduced themselves to Priya. It was clear that none of them knew what to expect next and how they were supposed to conduct themselves.

"Have you tried getting out of this place?" Priya croaked as she struggled to feel her dried and cracked lips. "I am parched. Is there something to drink here?" She suddenly started feeling thirsty as her senses started coming back.

"We have been scouring every inch of these four walls, and we haven't been able to spot any exit doors out of this room," John said. "Although there is no discernable exit, this place is stocked with enough food and water for us all to live here for many months, if not years. Whoever brought us here has planned this out meticulously. Let me get you some water." He walked across the room to the other side.

He walked up close to the wall on the other side, and the wall slid open smoothly to the side, revealing a dark room where the lights came on automatically as John entered the room. Even from across the cathedral-sized room, Priya could see racks of food, water and other supplies.

"Here you go! I've added some ice as well; that room has an ice machine." John extended the water glass towards Priya.

"Adjoining that room, there are two other rooms – one of them has six beds and the other has two full bathrooms. Going by this whole setup including the amount of food, the beds, and the bathrooms, it looks like whoever brought us here isn't intent on letting us out anytime soon," John continued.

"That is, if they intend to let us out of here in the first place!" Sanjeev exclaimed, trying not to show the anxiety in his voice.

"What is that large, black thing on that wall over there?" Priya asked John.

"That is a huge TV, which we haven't been able to turn on. Doesn't look like it is working. Although I suspect, just like everything else in this place, it is placed there for a reason. We just have to figure out how to make it work," John answered, trying to hide his admiration for the brains behind that place.

"Help me get up!" Priya grabbed John's hand and both of them walked up to the TV as others joined them as well. Just as the last of them stepped close to the TV, with a soft clicking sound, the dark TV screen lit up. Just then, a door in the floor slid open through which emerged what seemed like a reclining chair from the future.

The white chair looked like a high tech version of the dentist's chair, very comfortable with a head rest, while the clamps on arms and legs looked like they were designed to hold the person in position, and the sensor dials looked like the machine could measure heart rate, blood pressure, temperature, and brain activity as well.

"Umm, I took a few classes in forensic science and criminology. I think, based on the various sensors on it, that chair looks like a futuristic version of a plain old polygraph machine, that is used to detect whether someone is lying or telling the truth," Nagashree thought out loud.

Given the situation they found themselves in, they could not get themselves to trust each other fully. Any one of them could be the real kidnapper planted in the room as a mole.

"Ahmed! Are you alright??" Ranvir grabbed him as Ahmed was about to collapse.

"I need my insulin shot," Ahmed could barely speak, as Ranvir reflexively caught him and lowered him slowly to the floor while everybody else turned their attention to Ahmed.

"Where am I?" Those were the only words I could muster as I slowly opened my eyes and found myself on what seemed like a hospital bed with a bunch of intravenous pipes stuck to my limbs, and heart monitoring electrodes glued to my chest.

"Chaitu, I am so glad that you finally woke up. We were all so concerned about you." Didi came over and hugged me.

"How come you are here? When did you get here?" I was glad to see didi, but at the same time surprised as to when she'd flown over to Boston from India. Even though I couldn't recall how I ended up in the hospital, I could feel a lump in my throat and immense sadness and knew that something terrible had happened that landed me in the hospital.

"Krishna called me when they had to rush you to the hospital about a week back." Didi sat next to me and placed her hand on my forehead, gently brushing my hair back from my face.

"Have I been in the hospital for a week now?!" That caught me by surprise. It was the first time this had ever happened to me. I had lost all sense of time.

"You had a nervous breakdown and slipped into a coma." That's what the attending neurologist had diagnosed. "Your brain was trying to protect itself by shutting down," Didi tried to fill me in on what brought me to the hospital.

"Where is Zara?" I looked around, trying to see whether she was in the room.

"You don't remember, do you?" Didi asked looking at me with deep concern.

That was when the immense sorrow and sadness hit me, and all the memories came flooding back. Zara visiting Aleppo, her staying in the historic hotel in the old city, riots breaking out, and she and Narin getting caught up in the riots, and me reaching out to John Ratcliffe to help locate them and return them safely to the States.

"I need to call John. He must've located Zara and Narin by now," I tried to get out of the bed and get to the phone to call John.

"You already spoke with John, Chaitu." Didi tried to calm me and hold me down in bed.

"I did!" I was surprised as I had no recollection of it, but the lump in my throat got even bigger as I sensed that the news from John was not good.

"Yes. John's agent in Syria was able to locate Zara and Narin, and John was preparing to fly down there himself to bring them back to the States. In the meantime, the riots there intensified and there was a huge bomb blast in the building where Zara was hiding, and the whole building collapsed." Didi started crying uncontrollably. "There were no survivors from that blast," she continued between tears and sobbing.

My mind went blank. I did not feel anything. And I lost my will to live. There was no reason for me to get up or go anywhere or do anything. I did not know what to do with myself, as images of Zara kept flashing in my head – the first meeting in the grocery story to the last Skype call when she spoke excitedly about our baby's first kick.

Tears started rolling down my eyes, as didi hugged me tight. Not a word was said. She just sat there silently next to me, sobbing softly, as I drifted in and out of sleep and consciousness.

How does one move past such a thing? It was as if the ground had suddenly vanished from under me.

Knock! Knock!

There was a knock on the hospital room door, and as part of his morning rounds, the neurologist paid me a visit in my room. The moment he noticed that I was awake, he broke into a broad smile and exclaimed, "Good to have you back!"

"How are you feeling?" He went through the nurse's report from last night and reviewed my vitals.

"Your vitals look good. There was something in your brain MRI scan that I would like to take a deeper look at, just to ensure that you have a clean bill of health. We will keep you in the hospital for observation for another day, and you should be ready to go home by this time tomorrow," he continued.

Just as he was about to leave the room, he spoke softly, "I am deeply sorry for your loss."

The next day, as I was discharged from the hospital, Krishna came over to accompany didi and me on the drive back home.

"I don't think I can live anymore," I was mumbling to myself.

"You will have to find a way to live on. Know that you are not the only one who is experiencing such sorrow." Didi was always my pillar of strength and comfort. But it was annoying when she wouldn't just agree with me that I had to end it all right then. Neither she nor anyone could ever understand what I was going through right at that instance.

"The pain is so much that I wish I could go numb and not feel anything at all. I just want me to get away from me forever." There was no self preservation instinct left in me.

"Papa went through a lot of pain when mom died. He still managed to pull through and he never gave up," Didi would not let me go down that path.

"For me to continue living, I need to have a reason to get out of bed each day. And at this moment, I have none." I didn't believe at that point that there was anything that didi, or anybody else for that matter, could say that would change my mind.

"The reason for living will come to you. Give it time. Papa would not want you to quit, no matter how difficult life gets." Didi was certain about it. And I knew in my heart that she was right. I knew I would have to find a way to live on, for the memory of Zara, for papa, for didi, and for the gift of life itself.

"John and Priya, can you search through the food room and the fridge to look for insulin shots?" Ranvir spoke with a sense of urgency, as he tried to rest Ahmed's head on a pillow.

"Sanjeev, can you search the bedroom?" he continued.

"Nagashree, you are a doctor. You can stay by Ahmed, while I go search the bathrooms and the medicine cabinet, if there is one." Ranvir never lost his calm manner. He just seemed to know how to bring order to chaos without panicking or overreacting.

Nagashree came by Ahmed, who was starting to look very pale and was shivering, and took his pulse and checked his eyes. "He is going into shock. We need the insulin shot now!"

"Found them!" Priya shouted with palpable excitement, as she grabbed one from the fridge and darted back to Nagashree.

Nagashree took the injection from Priya and jabbed it into Ahmed's right thigh. Within a few minutes, Ahmed's complexion returned to normal and he wasn't shivering anymore.

"How often do you need this?" Priya asked Ahmed, as he recovered and propped himself up.

"Once every day," he responded.

"There were five shots in the fridge, including this one," Priya continued. "Assuming they've thought through everything, whoever brought us here intends to hold us hostage here for at least five days, if not more."

All of a sudden, the rush and excitement of addressing Ahmed's medical emergency was replaced by the realization that they all might be in this hostage situation for a very long time and may never ever get out alive.

"Come on, it is never as bad as we imagine it to be. Together, we will figure a way out to get out of here. I am certain." Ranvir was the first to break that silence and he knew how to inspire people and get them to focus on the positive things in life.

"Priya, did you see your kidnappers? Where were you when you were attacked?" Ranvir asked.

"Oddly enough, I did not see my kidnappers and I have no memory of being attacked," she replied.

"Is your last memory, before you woke up here in the body bag, that of attending an interview in Jaipur?" John asked Priya.

"Yes. How did you know that?" That caught her by surprise.

"The rest of us here share the same experience. On different dates and times, each of us had shown up for a job interview with the same internet company at Rajputana Hotel in Jaipur, and were ushered into the executive suite by a handsome man named Babloo. As we waited for the interview to begin, Babloo offered each of us a cool beverage and that is our last memory before waking up here, in this room," John summarized the experiences of the other five who had woken up before Priya.

"My experience is pretty much the same then. I remember drinking refreshingly cool watermelon juice that Babloo offered, as I was anxiously waiting for the interview to start," Priya concluded.

"I guess, based on such overwhelming evidence we can safely deduce that all of us have been kidnapped by either Babloo or the people associated with the internet company that invited us to the job interview," Sanjeev concluded.

"Have the kidnappers targeted us at random, or like everything else in this place, have we been specifically targeted and hence part of some higher order plan?" Ahmed finally joined in the hypotheses behind their kidnapping, after listening in quietly from the sidelines.

"In order to answer that question, we need to understand if there is anything else that connects us all," Ranvir spoke in a measured manner after having given it much thought. "Might be worthwhile to share our backgrounds to see if we are somehow connected," he continued.

"Seems like a sensible place to start the enquiry. Why don't you start it off," Priya had by now fully regained her composure and form.

"I will go first then," Ranvir replied. "My full name is Ranvir Iyengar. I grew up in Chennai, graduated in engineering from IIT Kharagpur, hold a doctorate in architecture with a focus on building environmentally friendly projects. I used to be the captain of the cricket team in college. I am married to Komal Iyengar, and both of us live in Ladakh. I have never been involved in any fights or major conflicts of any sort, and don't have any significant enemies," Ranvir paused.

"It could very well be the business owners in Ladakh, involved in water delivery using trucks. They might want me to stop the work that I have been doing to improve the water table in the region with artificial glaciers, as it impacts their lucrative business of delivering water through trucks. Also, another potential reason as to why I could be of interest to kidnappers is because my dad, Subramaniyam Iyengar, is a politician and Member of Parliament," Ranvir stopped speaking as his eyes went around the room, trying to gauge reactions from others, seeking any recognition of commonality with what he had just shared with them. After that, he looked at John to take it from there.

"My full name is John Verghese. I am a history major and my background is in municipality affairs management, including waste management and town planning. I grew up in Cochin and that is where I currently reside and work. I can't think of anything in my work or my personal life that would've led anybody to hate me enough to do something like this to me," John spoke looking at Ranvir. "I love technology and know a lot of facts, so have been on TV shows. Maybe somebody hated my looks or my voice," John was only half joking.

"I am Priya Pant. I grew up mostly in Delhi. I graduated from St. Stephen's College and work in the Civil Services division of the Indian Central Government, focused on public and economic policy. I have also been active in broader citizens' rights movements, including women's rights and gay and lesbian rights. As a result, I have received multiple threats in the past from political parties as well as religious groups. It could be anyone of those crazies who might be after me," Priya spoke looking at each of them. It was clear that this wasn't such a big surprise for her.

"Sanjeev Hegde," Sanjeev started off as Priya finished speaking. "I am an investigative journalist. I am no stranger to both fan mail and hate mail, so it could be anyone of those haters who might want to do this to me. And based on what I've heard so far, it looks like both Ranvir and Priya have similar backgrounds or at least reasonable causes to be candidates for some sort of political or religious vendetta. John, your background doesn't seem to fit that profile. So it begs the question as to who would want to hurt John as well," Sanjeev's mind was actively working to piece this puzzle together.

"Can you think of anything at all in your past that might

connect you to political or religious groups?" Sanjeev wondered looking at John.

"Hmm," John rubbed his forehead as he tried to reflect on his background. "One of the big events that was talked about in our house was the Pokhran nuclear test from the 70s. My dad, Sam Verghese, was the project manager taking care of the logistics of that effort," John responded to Sanjeev's query.

The mention of Pokhran and the nuclear test from the 70s lit up Sanjeev's face. "Aha, that might be it," Sanjeev stood up as if he seemed to have figured out this puzzle. "My mom, Rajni Hedge, was the main journalist from The Times of India covering the first Pokhran nuclear test. So John, that might be the link connecting you and me to this kidnapping," Sanjeev's mind was racing.

"I have heard so much about the nuclear test during our dinners, when I was a kid, that all the cast of characters and the events following the blast are permanently etched in my memory. Whenever my mom talked about it, there was a great sense of patriotic pride but she also had one regret that she didn't report, or at least investigate further, the potential radioactive fallout from the blast," Sanjeev's eyes glazed over as he recounted his memories from his childhood.

"She had seen the video footage of the blast, a few seconds right after the detonation, in which she had noticed a small cloud escape from the crater. Only one other person had noticed that cloud, and that was the chief scientist behind the whole effort. But it never got reported or investigated, buried under the patriotic euphoria that swept the nation right after the blast," Sanjeev continued on as more of those details came to his mind.

"And yes, the name of the chief scientist who had also noticed the radioactive cloud was Subramaniyam Iyengar," he paused as he suddenly realized that it is Ranvir's father.

"That is correct, Sanjeev. My dad was the chief scientist for the 'Smiling Buddha' nuclear test program," Ranvir confirmed Sanjeev's claim. "Unlike your mom, my dad didn't talk about it much when I was younger, and ever since he entered politics, he tried to distance himself from that test even more. And maybe that had something to do with that radioactive fallout."

"My dad, Narendra Pant was the army chief officer leading the 'Smiling Buddha' Priya interjected, clearly connecting her to Ranvir, John and Sanjeev.

"Srinath Reddy, my dad, was the cantonment area chief who authorized the use of the Pokhran test site for the nuclear blast," Nagashree added her connection to Pokhran.

"My father, Balbir Bakshi, was in charge of transferring the 'Smiling Buddha' bomb from Trombay to Pokhran in total secrecy," Ahmed pitched in.

"This might be stating the obvious, but it looks like all of us are connected to the Pokhran nuclear test in one way or another," Sanjeev's mind was in overdrive, making all these connections that just came to light.

As they discussed their kidnappers' motives, Ranvir got up and walked up to the white chair that had surfaced from the ground. "Maybe that polygraph chair holds the key to our escape from this place," he spoke, as if to himself.

"Hello," I finally called didi.

It had been more than six months since I had last seen didi when she was in Boston helping me recover from the coma. With each passing day, the pain and suffering from losing Zara had become less intense. Even though I wanted the pain to never dull in its intensity, sadly that was not going to be. I hated my mind for letting go of the memory of Zara despite my best efforts to the contrary.

"Hello, Chaitu. How are you doing?" Didi replied with concern in her voice.

"You were right. It did come to me – the reason for me to go on," I was thinking back on the conversation with didi during the ride back from the hospital.

"What is it?" she was cautiously curious, not wanting to derail anything that might have stabilized my mental makeup.

"Zara saw huge potential in Pokhran, a desert land, that can be rebuilt into a gleaming township that embraces Yazidi refugees and other refugees from around the world," I replied. "With right leadership, such a township can morph into much more than just a place to absorb refugees. It can be a pathway to a new Pokhran which will be good for the region and for the country as a whole." That desire to rebuild Pokhran gave me a new will to live and I had gone from barely breathing and surviving to meticulously planning and working through all my waking hours.

"That is a tall order. You need land, people to help, and also deal with the government bureaucracy. How will you manage to pull all that off?" Didi was always compassionate, but practical.

"On the land part, I am already ahead. Even before all this happened, as you are aware, I had been working on an internet ecommerce company based in India. For that company, I had already acquired about hundred square kilometres of unpopulated desert land near Pokhran. Roughly at about ten kilometres by ten kilometres, about twice the size of Manhattan, that land will be more than enough to build a free and progressive metropolis in the middle of the desert, which can be a beacon of hope for world refugees and a model of living that the rest of India can aspire for. This is what Zara would've wanted."

"I realize that I don't have enough time to be able to complete it all by myself, but at least I can get the ball rolling," I continued, addressing didi's concerns. "That is why I will be recruiting young, intelligent talent who also owe a debt to Pokhran. These will be the sons and daughters of the folks behind the Pokhran nuclear test."

"How will you get those people to work on this task? Will they even be interested in something like this?" Didi was quite sceptical.

"No. Very likely they won't be interested to do anything like this and especially at my behest, at least not at first blush. That is where I need your help to interview and recruit them, and train them in one of the underground warehouses that I had built for the ecommerce startup," I detailed out my grand plan.

"What if they don't take up your job offer?" Didi questioned.

"This won't be an optional offer. Living with Samarjit and Dada Saheb many years back taught me how to break hard-headed politicians by holding them in an enclosed cave for extended periods of time. I intend to do the same with these folks, until they agree to work on this task." I recognized at that point that I was playing with the line between good and bad, but I was counting on having the end justify the means.

After a long pause from the other end, "How can I help you?" Didi asked.

"I need you to interview six candidates. I have already identified those candidates, with Pokhran in their background, who have the right mindset and the capabilities to transform Pokhran. Based on their passions and what they've demonstrated so far in their life, they will be a great fit for the monumental task at hand.

One of them is an amazing leader who has already been driving positive change in Ladakh, another one is a fiery economist with a burning desire to radically transform how societies are organized, another one has been involved in developing special economic zones, and if we can get them to work together, then there is hope that Zara's dream of a gleaming Pokhran will come true," I continued.

"I will reserve an executive suite at Rajputana Hotel in Jaipur, where you will meet the candidates. Interview invites will go out to those candidates, requiring them to come to Rajputana and they will be expecting to meet you there," I provided details of how the candidates will be approached.

"As they show up for the interview, Babloo will slip them a safe dose of sleeping tablets. After that, he has his instructions to get those candidates over to one of the underground warehouses in Pokhran." I knew this was not the best approach, but I did not have the luxury of time on my side. Desperate times require desperate measures.

"Want to take a look at the 'truth chair' that we've been working on for you?" Krishna announced with a smile as he came into my living room.

Krishna and Rob had been working on an immersive virtual reality chair that would allow people to get the full experience of interacting with the virtual world that exists inside the computer. The chair would be loaded with sensors, that would keep track of the position and posture of the body along with the shape of each of the fingers and arms and legs so that it can be represented accurately in the virtual world, and actuators that can play back every interaction in the virtual world, such as a tree branch brushing against the player's arm, so the player can feel it in the real world.

The video gaming and social media companies had expressed a lot of interest in that chair as it had the potential to redefine the way people get to interact with others on the internet, making it almost a real life experience without leaving the comfort of their homes.

When they got to know the plan for rebuilding Pokhran, they offered to help in creating the 'truth chair', as Krishna liked to call it, that would detect whether the person seated in the chair was telling the truth or not.

As I wheeled myself into the lab, behind Krishna and Rob, we came up to what seemed like a large bed that was covered with a white sheet.

"There you go!" Krishna grabbed one end of the white sheet and pulled it off the chair with a dramatic flourish.

It looked like a torture chair from the future with loads of wires and sensors running around and underneath the chair. Although it was clearly far from a comfortable couch, that one can sink into as they play a videogame or browse their social media account, I was more interested to find out whether it was ready to confirm whether someone is telling the truth.

"Don't focus on the wires and the lack of cushion or comfort. We have a great design intern who has some cool ideas to greatly simplify this, and by the time she is done with it, this should look like a comfortable recliner or La-Z-Boy couch," Rob responded looking at the expression in my face, while Krishna was busy powering up the chair.

"I know you guys will take care of the aesthetics of the chair relatively quickly. All I want to know at this point is how well it works and how easy is it to operate," I voiced my concern, as that chair needed to be shipped to Pokhran within the next couple of weeks.

"Hey Rob, why don't you slip into the chair?" Krishna asked Rob, to give a demo of the chair.

As soon as Rob got into the chair, it was as if the chair came alive, with electrodes and clamps going around his feet, around his arms, around his fingers, and an electrode cap around his head.

"Now, all you need to do is ask him a yes or no question," Krishna continued with an impish smile.

"Do you want to ask the question?" he asked me.

"Why don't you do the honours! You seem to be excited to ask the question." I smiled back at Krishna.

"Rob, do you agree that Krishna is smarter than you?" Krishna asked Rob with a smile, knowing fully well that Rob would never admit to it.

Chapter 10
Rebuilding Pokhran
(2015-2019)

"Why are you being so difficult?" Ranvir asked, looking disapprovingly at Priya for being the only one to have failed the polygraph chair test the second time. Everybody else had cleared it this time, except for her. They were this close to getting out of the room.

Priya broke down and started crying, which came as a surprise to her as well. Maybe it was the stress of being locked up in that room or the fact that she was the only one that was holding them all back from getting out.

"I so desperately wanted to agree with you all," she spoke in between her tears. "But the chair is too sensitive, as it can detect even the slightest hint of doubt or lying in my mind. The only way for me to get past that chair is to share what is in my mind with all of you and hopefully you will agree with me."

Nagashree came over and sat next to Priya and placed her arm around her to comfort her, as Priya appeared to be the object of hate from others in that room.

"Over the past five days, the rest of us have all come to the general agreement that the best way to rebuild Pokhran for the twenty-first century is to base it on the founding principles of

America, that is life, liberty, and pursuit of happiness – hold human life sacred, zealously protect individual rights and freedom and allow individuals to act freely and take up things in their pursuit of happiness," Ranvir softened his tone as he realized that Priya was equally distraught at not clearing the polygraphic chair.

"What part of those principles do you have trouble agreeing with?" Ranvir knew they were running out of time. They had maybe twelve more hours before Ahmed would need his next insulin shot and they had used the last of those shots earlier that day.

"Why do you care so much whether you agree with others' ideas or not? Just stay cool and say 'yes' when you are seated in that chair," Sanjeev spoke looking at Priya, as he was sceptical of this whole thing right from the start. He wasn't convinced that they would ever be let out of that room by the kidnappers, and sitting on that chair and trying to answer some stupid question and being truthful at that seemed to border on the ridiculous.

"We have tried to fake our way past that machine before, Sanjeev. No point going that route again. Let's not try to take shortcuts and end up wasting more time. If the chair or the kidnappers want us all to agree on how to rebuild Pokhran, let us give it to them and hopefully get out of here and get on with our lives after that," Ranvir knew how to calm down Sanjeev while at the same time keep all of them moving forward.

"Go ahead, Priya. About time that you let us know what is it about those founding principles that you disagree with?" Ranvir directed his gaze at Priya and Nagashree as he spoke.

"I have no trouble with the first two principles – holding human life sacrosanct above all and protecting the rights and liberties of all the citizens," Priya started speaking softly at first, as she was acutely aware of the impatient glances trained on her. She also knew well this could end up becoming a heated discussion.

"It is the third principle – pursuit of happiness – that is flawed and carries within it the seeds for widening the chasm between the rich and the poor," Priya continued, as she looked across the room and began to take the lead in the discussion.

"That principle evokes such a strong reaction in me, that I ended up dedicating my post-graduate college work in economics focused on researching that principle. It had a lot to do with my father and his story of rags to moderate riches," as she spoke those words, there was pride in her voice for her father.

"Although I had a very privileged childhood with everything at my disposal that I could ask for, it wasn't the same for my father. He was orphaned at a very young age with no memory of his parents and grew up on the streets of Delhi. He remembers starving and weathering the cold Delhi winter nights on an empty stomach," Priya's eyes seemed to look into the distance and her voice was tinged with sadness as she spoke.

"The only thing that kept him alive and going on was the company and friendship of other orphans on the street. The kids watched out for each other, while nobody else did, and made sure that they shared amongst themselves equally any food that they found, stayed warm during nights and out of harm's way with the kids keeping watch in turns through the night," Priya continued as Sanjeev and John started fidgeting, waiting for her to make her point.

"It was there that he got a sense of belonging, that someone cared, and developed his leadership skills where he always looked at every situation as a win-win. He was fortunate enough to be picked up as a foot soldier for the army, which set him up on the path to success in life," she continued.

"The world is skewed in favour of those who have parents, and more importantly, those who have wealth and property from their parents,' he would always say. 'That is a win-lose situation, because those who inherit wealth and property get to win or succeed in life without having worked hard for it. And those who weren't fortunate enough to have parents or at least successful parents were destined to lose," she repeated her father's words.

"Persistence, patience and purpose – that is what I was led to believe to be the secret of success in life. Those parents worked hard and it should be alright for their kids to partake in the returns of their parents' hard work," Ranvir interjected.

"That is precisely what I have an issue with," Priya shot back right away, which caught everyone in the room by surprise. Nobody in the room was so curt to Ranvir, who had become like the elder brother to them all.

"Would you be fine if the inheritance of parental wealth and property were to be replaced with inheritance of loans and debt owed by the parents?" Priya asked, looking at Ranvir first and then the others in the room.

"That would be taking humanity back to the days of bonded labour," John, who was quiet till then, joined in the discussion as he had seen his grandfather fight against bonded labour in his village.

"Aha! Inheritance of parental loans and debt is not acceptable because that would be construed as bonded labour, which we all agree is evil and has no place in civil society," she paused as she took in a deep breath. "By the same measure, inheritance of parental wealth and property should be viewed as skewing the playing field," the tone of her voice became sharper as she emphasized the last part.

"For the sake of discussion, imagine life to be a running race where everyone is trying to reach their goal in the limited amount of time they have on this earth. In a fair race, everyone would start at the same starting point, which would only be possible if nobody moves the running blocks from their initial positions at the start of the race, giving everyone a fair chance to win the race," she started moving her hands in the air to visualize the running track and the starting blocks.

"By allowing inheritance of parental wealth and property to the kids, the society is making the race unfair, metaphorically speaking, by moving the starting blocks for such kids forward, giving them a significant head-start versus other kids that do not have the same level of inherited wealth," she paused at that point to look for reactions across the room.

"What is your point?" Sanjeev asked impatiently, as he just wanted everyone to pass the polygraph chair and hoped to get out of that place as soon as possible.

"Twenty-first century society should be creating a level playing field for all its citizens. Just as we abolished bonded labour and transfer of debt from parents to children in twentieth century, we should abolish inheritance in this century," Priya replied looking at Sanjeev.

After a long pause, Ranvir was the first one to speak. "Hmm. So, are you advocating that the founding principles should be life, liberty and level playing field for all?" Ranvir asked almost making a statement. Despite his initial reservations, the notion that inheritance is just another side of the much-reviled bondedthat inheritance is just another side of the much-reviled bonded labour resonated with his own sentiments about creating a society where everyone had truly equal opportunities.

"Yes," Priya was quick to respond, and there was no indecision or uncertainty in her voice.

"I have to get out of this place. I can't take being cooped up inside this place any longer," Ahmed jumped into the white polygraph chair, ready to take on whatever it had to dish out.

It was as if like the chair suddenly became alive. While the others looked on with shock and trepidation, the chair clamped down on Ahmed's arms, legs and across his chest, making it impossible for him to move or to get off it.

Sensors wrapped around both his index fingers. Electrodes attached themselves around his head, temples, and forehead. "Ahmed, do you agree with the others in the room?" a mechanical voice boomed from the speakers embedded in the chair.

"This is your first of three chances," the voice continued in a monotone. "Don't try lying. That is not going to work. The sensors will record your heartbeat, your blood pressure and your brain activity to know whether you are telling the truth," the voice went on, as Ahmed began to sweat.

"You have five minutes to respond with a yes or no," the voice stopped as all the sensors attached to Ahmed went online all at once, sending a bluish soft aura around his body, wherever the sensor came in contact with his skin.

Right at that time, the TV screen lit up and in big bold letters, that filled the large screen, was the question:

Do you agree with the others on how to rebuild Pokhran?

"Ahmed, you should've waited a bit more before jumping on to the chair. We all will have a very different take on the question. There is no way you will be able to convincingly answer that question without having discussed with us first and there is no way in hell that we can cover that topic in the next five minutes," Sanjeev chided Ahmed for being so impatient.

"Ow!!" John let out a small scream, as he was thoroughly scrutinizing the technology behind the chair trying to find a way to extract Ahmed out of the tough situation that he landed himself in. "Not to stress you out even more Ahmed, but the back of the chair seems to be equipped with a lethal injection, going by the label in the back of the chair."

"Everyone, for the next few minutes, let's focus on getting Ahmed safely out of this chair," Ranvir tried to get everybody else to think of ways to help Ahmed out of his current predicament.

Nagashree tried to pry open the clamps around Ahmed's wrists as Sanjeev tried to break the clamps around his feet.

"This bloody thing is built like a rock. There is no way to break this apart," all of them agreed.

"Looks like the only option left for you, right now, is to try to answer the chair's question. Maybe you will manage to fool those sensors," Ranvir tried to be as soothing and calm as possible, trying not to rattle Ahmed's nerves any further.

At that point, everyone in that room went dead quiet, as Ahmed was about to speak.

"Yes!" Ahmed took a deep breath and tried to relax his entire body as he replied to the question from the TV and the chair.

The sensors in the chair went into an overdrive with beeping sounds and blinking sensor lights till that same mechanical voice came on, as everyone held their breath.

"You lied. You have two more chances." As soon as the voice finished that statement, with a big hissing sound, all the clamps around Ahmed opened up and he jumped out of that chair.

"Are you alright?" Nagashree asked Ahmed as he regained his composure.

"Except for my heart beating like crazy, I am otherwise fine," Ahmed replied looking at Nagashree, as the rest of the others waited for his response.

"Two things are clear to me now," Sanjeev broke the silence as he took stock of their situation. "Firstly, that chair is very likely our door to the outside world, as I don't see any other path that is available to us," he continued.

"Secondly, we will have to discuss that TV question together and all of us have to agree from the bottom of our hearts about how we would rebuild Pokhran," he paused, as he blurted out without much thought, "regardless of whether we care enough about Pokhran or not."

"He is right. To get past those sophisticated sensors, the only way is to tell the truth," Nagashree added.

"And that means we all have to be on the same page which might prove to be much harder than it seems on the surface, given our different religious and cultural backgrounds," Nagashree continued.

"These kidnappers must have very twisted and cruel minds. This entire setup and especially that chair is designed to be extreme torture. When I get out of here, I am going to go after our kidnappers and make sure that they pay for what they've put us through here." Ahmed was seething with anger as he recovered from his trip to the chair.

"Although, if you look at the intent of the kidnappers, which is to rebuild Pokhran, that seems to be squarely in the good territory." John could only see things objectively and in a fact based manner.

"Are you now on the side of the kidnappers? Maybe you are one of them?" Ahmed was visibly pissed at John for even hinting that the kidnappers could potentially have good intentions.

"Okay guys. Let's not fight amongst ourselves. Based on what Sanjeev said earlier, we will have to work together. It can't be that hard to get past that chair," Ranvir stepped in, trying to break the tussle between Ahmed and John.

"Folks, how about not doing anything here at all. If we just wait long enough, our folks in the outside world might be able to find us and get us out of here," Sanjeev offered an alternative to sitting on the chair and going through the charade of answering the question on TV. "I have been gone for more than twenty-four hours now and knowing my mom, she won't just stay put without doing anything. She will create a media frenzy that is bound to mobilize the police authorities to take action," Sanjeev sounded confident that his mother would not rest until he was freed.

"In case nobody comes to rescue us, bear in mind that we have at most four days before we run out of insulin shots for Ahmed. We got to at least try and reach consensus before that," Ranvir spoke as everybody else, including Sanjeev, nodded in agreement with that.

"Hmm. Levelling the playing field and requiring people to abdicate their wealth and property to the society instead of bequeathing to their kids," Sanjeev paused as he paraphrased where Priya was headed with the founding principles. "That runs counter to anything that we observe in nature."

"Every species, including us humans, is here because its parents were willing to put in the hard work and whatever sacrifice it took to ensure the survival of their off-springs. It is in our basic animal nature to protect and provide for our young ones," Sanjeev tried getting his head around the idea of people giving up their property to the society instead of to their kids.

"Black lace-weaver spider mothers, found in Americas and Europe, make the ultimate sacrifice with their bodies and their lives as they offer themselves up to be nutritious food for their young hatchlings. After the young ones hatch, mothers could readily leave their web, but instead they encourage their young ones to feed on their bodies," John jumped in, almost as an involuntary reaction.

"Moreover, anywhere in the world, if someone were to choose to not bequeath their wealth and property to their children, they can very well do so. Nobody will stop them. They don't need everybody in the society to do the same thing with their wealth. Nothing prevents your parents from cutting you off from any inheritance, if you so wish," Sanjeev took a personal shot at Priya in an attempt to get her to capitulate her stance.

"Just because it happens in nature, and we humans might have similar basic instincts, doesn't mean that we have to be a slave to those instincts. For example, in most civil societies now, we no longer fight to death when men are vying for a woman's attention, even though that is still the case in the animal world," Priya responded in a slow measured manner, looking at Sanjeev.

"Another more relevant counterexample is democracy itself, which goes against the basic instincts to hoard power and control observed in the animal kingdom," she continued. She had been attacked with such questions for far too long, and knew well how to handle them.

"Imagine you are thrown back in time, by about two thousand five hundred years back, to around 500 BC." She stood up and slowly started pacing in front of the others. "Everywhere you look, there are kings or queens ruling their monarchies with an iron fist or there are smaller tribes with chiefs who are no different in their tyranny and thirst for power from the kings or queens of bigger nations or kingdoms. There is no peaceful transition of power from one ruler to the next, unless the next ruler is the heir to the throne. Common man has no representation in the governance of the society and everybody's potential is limited, and dictated, by what the king or the queen or the tribal chief wants them to do." She stopped pacing and turned around to face the others.

"Cleisthenes in Athens faced that exact situation just like many other kings and chiefs before him. He looked to the animal world for inspiration on how best to govern Athens so that the constant power struggles and bloody murders could be replaced with more peaceful and productive governance for all the citizens of Athens." She resumed her pacing again, as it had been her habit while giving her lectures.

"He looked at animals that had evolved to live in large groups or communities. From his perspective, bee colonies and ant colonies appeared very close in their structure to human societies of that time. Both those colonies are solely geared towards the nourishment and care of the queen bee or ant, and do not place similar importance on the well-being of the other members of those colonies. He knew that would not work for his Athens," she continued while making eye contact with the others to make sure that they were following along. "Great people see and face the same things as others do, but they react to them differently than others," she made that statement and paused so that it had its intended effect on others.

"Cleisthenes saw the same situation, as other kings or queens before him saw, but he decided to handle it differently. More importantly, he understood that people have trouble tearing down something that they helped build or put in place. He surmised that if people had an equal stake in making the ruling decisions for Athens, they would be equally vested in them and work towards supporting and enforcing those decisions rather than trying to subvert those decisions," she continued painting the picture of ancient Athens with Cleisthenes developing a transformational governing structure.

"His solution, to the constant power struggles and exiles or murders, was to form an assembly of all free men of Athens, where each man got one vote. These men would then meet regularly in the afternoon, on a small hill top in the shadow of the Acropolis, to discuss and vote on all aspects of Athens, from the price of grain and olives to the raising of taxes and declarations of war. That was the first time in history where every man, king, noble or common man, got equal representation in the decision-making process for their country or city. Cleisthenes' reforms revolutionized all aspects of Athenian life, almost immediately. They ushered in an era of unparalleled achievement and prosperity as they released untapped potential among the citizens of Athens." She paused and took a deep breath, as she herself felt proud at such an amazing accomplishment by folks from so far back in the past.

"Democracy was thus born. And even after two thousand five hundred years, it is still a constant struggle to stop tyrants and the greedy power mongers from taking over the reign of democracies and instituting their will onto the population through monarchies or dictatorships. If Cleisthenes could level the governing landscape, making it possible for all citizens to have fair and equal representation in the matters of the State, so far back and transform the way we live now, then we should be able to level the playing field for all citizens of Pokhran, as they start out on their life's journey after leaving their parents' nest. So that every citizen has equal access to all opportunities, unencumbered by those who would've otherwise taken up more resources simply because they inherited wealth and property from their parents. That will usher in an era where every person has a fair shot at reaching their true potential," she concluded. She could see strong nods of acknowledgement and smiles from Ranvir and Nagashree, and knew she had won them over. She knew that Sanjeev would be a tough one to crack, but she was up for the challenge. She knew she was on the right side of the argument and was willing to fight for it.

As Sanjeev had predicted, within twenty-four hours, his mother created a media frenzy for her missing son, mobilizing the police into action. The authorities in Delhi and Jaipur joined forces to create a coordinated task force to track down the whereabouts of the six people who seemed to have been kidnapped from the same place in Jaipur, who had all been invited there for job interviews.

"Hey, look at that, the TV seems to show us the news of the outside world whenever I press this button at the bottom," John sounded excited to finally see something that broke the monotony of being imprisoned.

"Oh, that is my mom speaking to the media reporters. They are all looking for us now. It shouldn't be too long before they find us and get us out of here," Sanjeev spoke, clearly proud of his mother.

"Maybe we can send out messages or email through that thing?" Priya asked John who seemed to be good with the technological stuff.

"Doesn't seem to be a way, I have already tried. We can only receive information from the internet but can't send messages back out," John replied.

"Sanjeev, if they track us and free us, then that would be a great outcome," Ranvir knew how to prioritize and keep everybody focused on what was truly important.

"Let us work with the assumption that they won't be able to track us. I suspect that our kidnappers, who seem to have thought about everything, would have taken steps to throw the police off as well," he continued, convinced that they would have to find a way out of there themselves.

They had been discussing and debating these things over the past five days, quickly realizing that even among six people, there could be such deep differences of opinion. The stakes were high and their very survival depended on working together and coming to an agreement. The fear of the polygraph chair certainly raised the bar for the level of agreement they all needed to achieve. They all knew that they could not fake agreement.

Each of them was highly opinionated and given their different religions, socio-economic backgrounds, level of patriotism and their worldview, coming to an agreement amongst themselves proved to be more like a game of snakes and ladders, with one step forward followed by two steps back.

There was ready agreement on things that were more visible and which on the surface seemed important such as how to plan the city, how to keep it green, what sort of businesses and industries to promote and what basic facilities or infrastructure to build. Disagreements and trouble started when Priya asked what seemed like a basic question, "What will be the core founding principles of Pokhran?"

Given her background in public policy and economics, Priya understood the impact of founding principles of countries and their eventual success in providing a nurturing society that enables each of its citizens to pursue and reach their true potential.

"Do we really have to go down to that level of detail for the question that the chair is asking?" Ahmed dreaded the possibility of being stuck in that warehouse, and this question from Priya had the potential to stir up a lot of passionate debate and even more disagreement among that group.

"If any question is important to Priya or to anyone of us, we will have to address that in order to get past that chair. There is no sliding such things under the carpet, as those electrodes will sense even such subtle uncertainties in our heads." Nagashree wanted to make sure everybody understood how sophisticated those sensors could be.

"Haven't we tried levelling the playing field for all citizens with communism, where nobody is allowed to accumulate wealth? And we know now, after the collapse of Soviet Union and other communist countries, that such a construct and society will fail because it takes away motivation and ambition from people." The sceptic in Sanjeev wasn't convinced that this had never been tried before.

"No." Priya was clear that what she and her research advisors in the outside world proposed had not been tried before, at least not in any known society thus far. "Citizens of the society will have full freedom to pursue their passions and work as they choose and accumulate as much wealth and property as possible, within the confines of the laws of the society. In that regard, it will be a capitalist democracy, very similar to India or America, and it won't be anywhere close to communism," she answered.

"What they can't do is pass on their accumulated wealth to the next generation. Every generation will have to start from more or less the same starting point as everybody else in the society, as they won't be able to rest on the laurels and achievements of their parents," she paused and looked across the room, as she noticed Ahmed also starting to nod in agreement along with Ranvir and

Nagashree.

"In the current day capitalist democracies, the gap between the haves and the have-nots has the potential to become an uncrossable chasm, as the gap continues to grow and become wider with each passing generation," Priya continued.

"By levelling the playing field and moving wealth and property to the State instead of passing on to the children, the gap between the haves and have-nots will only be limited to a single generation, as it will be reset with every new generation," she concluded.

"No matter what we do, there will be a large portion of the poor population at the bottom that will support a small portion of the rich at the top. This has gone on since time immemorial and there is no fix for it," Sanjeev interjected.

"Hmm. Priya's concept of levelling the playing field, although not a perfect fix, comes close to offering a practical fix to that problem that has gone on for centuries. There are quite a few examples from history, where attempts were made to bridge that gap between haves and have-nots, including the nationalization of ancestral property in India after Independence and formation of Israel. In all those examples, the central flaw was that it was a one-time only effort. They did not consider resetting the gap on a periodic basis," John spoke at length. Priya started smiling and was glad to finally have John support her argument with his facts.

"Can the parents still pay for their kids' college and provide for their kids after they are grown?" John asked trying to understand how this would work in practice.

"Parents provide for them till they reach twenty-one years. After twenty-one, each individual will have to make their own living and fend for themselves. And those who are incapable of working will be supported by the State, similar to the social welfare services that currently exist. Except that the state will have potentially greater funds to be able to help those that can't help themselves," she replied, recognizing that any number for the age cut-off is arbitrary at this point only serving an illustrative purpose.

"As they say, the road to hell is paved with good intentions. Despite all the merits, the devil is in the implementation. How will the playing field be levelled in practice?" Sanjeev asked, trying to get in sync with Priya's line of thinking.

"Any help parents can provide will stop once the kids reach twenty-one years of age. The kids can't receive any gifts of land, houses, gold or bank accounts from their parents. The kids of parents with greater wealth and property will still get access to the network of successful and accomplished members of the society, which gives those kids greater advantage than the others who don't have access to a similar network. Hence it is not the perfect solution, but still comes pretty close to being perfect." Priya was happy to see that Sanjeev had gone past the whys and was now focused on the hows, which in her experience meant that he had practically crossed over to her side.

"What happens to all the wealth that the parents had accumulated in their lifetime?" John asked his final question.

"It will go to the government as tax revenue, which will be used towards defence, to build infrastructure such as roads, bridges and hospitals, and to provide basic facilities such as education, power, subsidies to farmers, and whatever else might require the state's attention and funding," she explained.

Chapter 11
Chaitanya's Letter from Beyond
(2019)

"I am going to track down Ranvir myself. The police here is too slow to do anything. Plus, I can't stay here doing nothing while my husband is out there suffering," Komal called her parents, letting them know that she was headed out to the deserts of Rajasthan.

"Do you know anything about the whereabouts? The police is already on the task to find the kidnappers based on all the news in the media," Komal's mom was concerned for her daughter's safety. But she also knew that once Komal had made up her mind, there was nothing she could say that would stop Komal from going ahead with her plan.

"Ranvir and I had turned on GPS tracking for both our phones. So I know where his phone is and he knows where my phone is, at any point of time. The last coordinates of Ranvir's phone, which went dead about twelve hours back, are about fifty kilometres south-east of Jaisalmer, in a tract of barren desert land. Based on what I could pick up from the online maps, there are no houses or buildings near those coordinates," Komal replied, providing more details.

"I know I can't stop you. So please be careful and call me every day," Komal's mom responded.

Komal coming out to track Ranvir was something I had not

anticipated.

I had instructed Babloo to properly dispose of their cell phones so that nobody could track them. Babloo had buried the cell phones in the middle of nowhere in the desert so as to throw the police completely off track.

She obviously loved him enough to drive all the way from Delhi on the same night that Ranvir was kidnapped. He was supposed to call her that night, and when he didn't, she suspected something was not right and started out to the point of his last cell phone signal.

They were married for a little over a year. Ranvir was everything to her and she could not imagine a life without him in it. She was determined to track him and return him to safety, if that was the last thing she would do in this life. Hardly was she prepared to drive and survive in the desert, and the spot where Babloo had buried the phones was very remote, many miles from any habitation.

By the time she reached that spot, her vehicle's engine was filled with fine sand that clogged up the carburettor and it stopped working. After a couple of days in the desert without water and food. She was disoriented and lost. In her confused state, she overstepped the line of control with Pakistan and was shot by a sniper from the other side. Once I got to know that Komal was out there looking for Ranvir, I asked Babloo to try to track her down and bring her back to safety. Babloo tried to get to her as fast as he could, but it was already too late.

The newspapers and TV channels got wind of Komal's death and as the circumstances of her death were unclear, they blamed it on the kidnappers.

News about Komal's death flashed on the large screen in the warehouse, and for Ranvir, that was all happening too fast. He didn't expect Komal to go looking for him, nor did he expect the kidnappers to go after Komal. And now to see that she was shot and found dead in the desert was very surreal. He didn't know how to react.

Everybody else went silent, not knowing how to console Ranvir. Priya and Nagashree came over and hugged Ranvir. The usually composed and self-assured Ranvir was reeling in shock.

"I have to get out now. I will have to take out those who were responsible for this!" Ranvir's voice was cold and emotionless, but it sent a shudder down everybody else's spine.

"Do we have consensus? Let's try getting on that bloody chair and get this over with," he was clearly seething inside and everyone nodded in agreement.

First one to go on the chair was Priya and as the mechanical voice finished asking the question, Priya responded with "yes" and the chair confirmed that she was telling the truth.

The last one to go on the chair was Ranvir, who by that time had regained his composure. If he was hurting or furious, that didn't show on his face anymore. And he responded with a "yes" to the question from the chair and the chair confirmed that he was telling the truth.

As soon as Ranvir got off the chair, there was a big rolling sound, and the entire wall started moving up, slowly revealing a passage way that lead into the cargo bay of a long container truck. The moment they all walked into the container cargo bay, the doors of the bay shut down and the truck started moving at great speed.

After about an hour of driving, the driverless truck came to an abrupt stop and the doors of the cargo bay flung open, revealing bright sunlight and dry desert sand for as far as the eyes could see.

And just like that, they were free. Free to go back to their interrupted lives, and other than the truck, there was nothing by way of clues as to who was behind all this.

It took them a few hours to get to a working phone. As soon as they placed the phone call, they were surrounded by media and the police.

Once the dust settled and the others were heading back to their lives, Priya asked, "Are you going to be fine, Ranvir? Would you like me to stay with you?"

"I am going to be alright. No, you should go ahead. I just have to find out who was behind Komal's death," he replied.

"I won't be able to understand what you must be going through. But two wrongs don't make a right. Why not let the authorities go after the kidnappers?" she spoke with grave concern in her voice.

"This is something I have to do. You should get back to your life," there was finality in his voice and Priya knew that there was nothing she could do or say at this point that Ranvir would be willing to listen to.

As the newfound friends bid their goodbyes, Ranvir headed straight to Rajputana and to the executive suite where this whole thing began. He wasn't sure whether he would find anything or anybody there, but that was where he would start and work his way from there.

Ranvir was surprised to find Babloo, still staying at that same suite. Without much of a fight or resistance, Babloo offered up the whereabouts of the kidnappers. Ranvir grabbed the gun from Babloo as he headed out to meet face to face with his kidnappers.

The voice in the back of Ranvir's head kept thinking that this was all way too easy and that it must be a trap. But he did not care as he had nothing to lose. He had to do this, as the thought of torturing and killing the kidnappers was what gave him a reason to breathe and to live for now.

It was a disappointingly nondescript house, at the outskirts of Pokhran, that Babloo's directions led him to and as he flung open the door, he saw a frail figure seated in the wheelchair.

"What took you so long, Ranvir?" the figure in the wheelchair asked calmly, as Ranvir stood there, his blood boiling with anger at this man that had taken his Komal away from him. As his hatred and rage took over, he found himself in a trance where all that mattered to him was to kill this man seated in that wheelchair as he raised his gun and took aim and shot at Chaitanya, sending him rolling to the floor.

Cold front coming down from the north had dumped a couple of feet of snow across the campus, covering the low hanging arches and the otherwise shiny moat that goes all the way around the Chapel. Nestled between Kresge Auditorium and two groves of london plane trees, stripped bare by the winter and the recent snow, the windowless cylindrical building with its textured red brick exterior stood out in sharp contrast to the white powdery snow around. With its non-denominational character and lack of affiliation to any one religion, the MIT chapel seemed like the perfect place, if ever is one for holding memorial service, to hold Chaitanya's memorial service.

Despite the cold and the snow, a large crowd had gathered in the chapel dressed in long black coats and hats, including members of the faculty, Chaitanya's past and current students, members of the Yazidi council, and others that got to know Chaitanya over the years. With a seating capacity of about hundred, the chapel was too small to accommodate the crowd that was starting to arrive. It pretty soon turned into standing room only situation with folks gathering around outside to pay their respects to the one that had departed.

Inside its windowless interior, on a raised platform in the middle of the altar was a large picture of Chaitanya. Right behind the altar, the tall metallic structure with its reflecting plates provided a backdrop that gave one a sense of ascension upwards toward the sky through the circular opening in the ceiling. Despite explicit instructions to the contrary from Chaitanya, Krishna and Rob organized the memorial service to honour the passing of their friend of over thirty years.

"It feels like only yesterday that Krishna and I picked up Chaitanya from the Logan airport. Most of you gathered here already know of his accomplishments both in the academia and in the business world, so I won't spend time going through them. Moreover, if he were here, he would totally forbid me from focusing the spotlight on him," Rob spoke standing behind the podium.

"Relentless desire for the service of others, his love of complexity, and his unbridled optimism were the traits that defined Chaitanya. Every major decision in his life was weighed against the value it creates for others and for society than for himself. I remember clearly the mental anguish he went through while deciding to sell his nuclear fission modelling software to Northrop Grumman, as he wanted to ensure that it created value and didn't add to more destruction. Most people, especially in our capitalistic society, believe that pursuit for individual wealth and glory will lead to career success and eventually happiness in life. Through his life, Chaitanya demonstrated that pursuit of greater good can and will lead to career success and not the other way around," Rob paused as he looked up from the notes he had scribbled on the paper. He was never comfortable with public speaking, but today, that fear seemed to be completely gone.

"He was truly gifted in his love of complexity. His ability to gravitate towards large problems – be it the development of simulation models that can predict outcomes of large events like nuclear explosions or the processing of mountains of data that we all generate daily through our social media interactions including tweets, blogs, messages – and make sense out of them to provide practical uses was truly a gift we were lucky to be a part of. I am certain, Krishna will agree with me when I say, that both of us would not have achieved our career and material success if we didn't have the good fortune to meet and work with Chaitanya." Rob looked at Krishna, who was nodding with tears in his eyes, as he spoke. He was about to choke, overcome with sudden sadness, but controlled himself.

"He would have been the first one to tell me that what I am about to say is corny, in his heavy Indian accent. Being with him, I learned how to stop complaining and start living a happy life. It is not so much what he said, but how he used to live that opened up my mind. There was so much that he had gone through in his life – be it his physical condition or the loss of his loved ones at different stages in his life. Any single one of those events would have been enough to bring down the strongest amongst us. But none of that stopped him from smiling and getting up to face life the next day. He was hope and optimism personified and I am happier because of him," Rob folded and placed the note with his scribbles in his upper left coat pocket, as he concluded his speech.

As Rob walked down from the podium, there were a few claps, mostly from current students of Chaitanya, but then it died down as people weren't sure, as no one is ever sure how to conduct themselves at a funeral. Krishna, who was the master of ceremony for the memorial service, came up to the podium.

"You know, you didn't have to hold back your applause. That would've been perfectly fine with Chaitanya, as he would often say 'Krishna, both life and death should be celebrated'. Whenever the topic of death came up in our discussions, he would mention one of the tribes around present day Iran, from Herodotus' History of the World, who would hold a happy celebration whenever one of their own passed away. They did that not out of disrespect for the dead, but rather from the belief that death is a happy and joyous culmination to a life that was well lived. And Chaitanya certainly did that in his life," Krishna spoke as he addressed the gathering once he got onto the podium.

"Now I would like to invite Radhika, Chaitanya's older sister, to say a few words. We are all very glad that she could join us here today, all the way from Pokhran, Chaitanya's hometown in India," he stepped off the podium as Radhika walked towards it.

Radhika stood there, a strong but diminutive figure at five feet two inches, while Krishna lowered the microphone.

"Events chose Chaitanya. He did not choose them," Radhika started to speak, without a hint of hesitation, because her mind was flooded with emotions. She fought hard to hold back tears as she knew that her Chaitu would not want her to shed tears or to feel sad for his death.

"He wanted his death to be a day of celebration and not one of sorrow. Despite my heavy heart, I shall make every attempt to speak about the positivity and optimism in my Chaitanya's life," she continued.

"I was ten years old when I first held Chaitanya in my arms, as he was born. That was both the happiest and the saddest day of my life. Our mother died during childbirth, so I ended up being both his mother and his sister," she paused as she looked up and across the room.

"He was a happy kid, full of tireless energy. He kept me busy and filled our house with much needed joy and happiness," she continued. "For over forty years, he has been my little brother and my best friend. And to see him pass away before me is the saddest thing in my life, and it is something that I wouldn't wish on even my worst enemies," she spoke as her eyes welled up.

"Chaitanya had the uncanny ability to get to the heart of the problem. It was just the way he viewed the world around him. Most people get mad at the motorist that cuts onto their path as the motorist was trying to avoid a pothole on the road, just because that is all their eyes and their mind can readily see. Instead, Chaitanya believed that the right target for their anger should be the municipality head or the official who was responsible for the construction and maintenance of the roads in that area." She was determined to talk about things that were important to Chaitanya.

"Whether it was the murder of our father by politicians, for trying to uncover the truth behind the nuclear fallout from the nuclear test, or the death of his friend Samarjit at the hands of the police, he could never get angry at the immediate perpetrators of those heinous acts as he perceived those to be symptoms. He knew that the media did not do its job of reporting the truth about the nuclear test, and the botched efforts at nationalization of lands led to vigilante leaders like Samarjit who took matters into their own hands to provide justice to the poor and the oppressed. He wanted to fix the root causes, not just treat the symptoms," she continued with clear pride in her voice for what Chaitanya stood for and believed in.

"Every hardship that was thrown at him only made him stronger and more resolute to find meaning and purpose for his life, despite all odds. From a shy child he grew up to be a strong personality, one who could take on complex problems and solve them, by the time he landed here at MIT at a mere sixteen years," she paused, as a murmur went across the hall at the mention of Chaitanya arriving at MIT at sixteen.

"Once he made up his mind, he did not quit, no matter how difficult the task," she resumed as the murmur died down. "He was most happy ever since he met Zara. She was the love of his life. And when she was taken away from him during the Syrian riots, he knew that the heart of the problem lay in the fact that the Yazidi people do not have a place that they can truly call home. If they did, then Zara would still be alive," Radhika spoke with affection for Zara, as she reflected back on her time with Zara visiting the market in Jaipur. "It was a combination of those events that provided the motivation behind his efforts to rebuild Pokhran both as a place for refuge for Yazidis, in memory of Zara, and as a place where everyone could be free to follow their dreams and reach full potential. He wanted me to share that with anyone who might be able and willing to help in that cause. It would've made him happy to know that I got to share his message here today with you all." She recognized that this gathering was as close to a perfect place as possible to share the message and get support for Chaitu's cause.

"Even in his death, he didn't quit. Papa would've been proud to know that," Radhika concluded with a smile, as she remembered young Chaitanya struggling to get up on that dining chair with Paramvir waiting and watching from the corner.

As she walked off the podium, applause broke out across the chapel and amongst those who were gathered outside in the bitter cold. The applause continued for a long time and smiles broke out as everyone took cues from Radhika to treat Chaitanya's memorial service as a day of celebration and joy, and not one of sadness or sorrow.

ONE MONTH LATER

As Ranvir was about to step out, he noticed a large package right outside his door. Inside it was a letter from Chaitanya.

Dear Ranvir,
If you are reading this letter, then I must already be dead.

I understand if you are still mad and angry with me for what I have done. I take full responsibility and the blame for kidnapping you, but I had no intention of harming Komal or anybody else in the process. Despite the news and media accounts, it was not I who killed Komal, although I did not deny it when you came after me with that gun. Thank you for putting me out of my misery.

At this point, if you are feeling any guilt for killing me, please don't. When I slipped into a coma after losing Zara, the doctors diagnosed me with late stage brain cancer. If you didn't shoot me, the cancer would've killed me by now anyway, except that it would have been a lot slower and more painful death.

My lawyers should have already taken care of ensuring that my death is not connected to you in anyway, so that you don't have to ever look over your shoulder expecting the police or somebody to come after you.

Out of the six of you, I chose to send this letter to you because if anyone can rebuild Pokhran and provide asylum to even a few Yazidi people, that will be you. You are a natural leader, are compassionate and have immense patience and persistence to cut through all the opposition that will come out of the woodworks in a country like India. You have already demonstrated that through the artificial glacier initiative in Ladakh.

No, you do not have to start from scratch. I am leaving in your capable hands a hundred square kilometres of desert land near Pokhran, the warehouses, and one thousand crores which should be enough to get you started and hire all the resources you need.

The land and the money is yours, no strings attached. Although my fond hope is that you will decide to use it towards rebuilding Pokhran not only because it offers you a way of giving back for the nuclear test, that your father was a part of, but also gives you a reason to live again.

I believe the founding principles – life, liberty, and level playing field – that the six of you developed and agreed to in the closed room are the right ones to form the basis for building a progressive society in Pokhran.

It is certainly not going to be easy, but nothing worth doing ever is.

Also, I don't expect Pokhran to offer asylum to every refugee, rather only to those that agree to the founding principles. And towards that end, you will have access to the polygraphic chairs that can be your border control and immigration check tools, so that you can use those to extend residency only to open and freethinking individuals that truly agree with the founding principles. Krishna and Rob have volunteered to help with the polygraphic chairs in the future, if you decide to use them. They are the real brains and innovators behind developing those chairs and they will be more than happy to help you in this endeavour.

Zara was passionate about building a well-planned city, something that can rival Las Vegas in USA, on that ten kilometre-by-ten kilometre tract of land near Pokhran, that will come into your possession. She had developed detailed town plans that I've left with the lawyers. In case you decide to use them, you will notice that the streets and the roads in those plans are perfect straight lines that cut at right angles. That grid pattern of streets is something that would've made my father happy, as he was impressed with similar construction in Germany during his visit there, and as he would say, it gives the town a sense of a much larger place than it actually might be.

No matter how you decide to go forward, it will be your decision and I wish you well in whatever direction you choose to go.

As for me, I know I am going to be joining the love of my life, and for that I shall forever be grateful to you. All I ever wanted was to make Zara happy and to make a difference in the lives of people living in Pokhran.

With the best of wishes,
Chaitanya

As he finished reading the letter, Ranvir felt a tear roll down his cheek. He had never thought he would feel anything but anger towards his kidnapper, but this letter changed everything. And for the first time since Komal's death, he felt hope again and a reason to live as he picked up the phone to call Priya, John and others to head towards Pokhran. As he hung up the phone, he stepped out into a bright sunny day with a smile on his face and only three words on his lips – "Let's rebuild Pokhran!"

A note from the author

The main objective behind writing this novel was to inform the general population about Paracracy (par → equal (Latin) and kratia → rule (Greek)), which is a new term coined to capture a novel form of government and a novel way to structure societies to eradicate generational build-up of the wealth gap. In a Paracratic society, almost everything will be maintained as in the current day democracies with free markets, with one change being that citizens will not be bequeathing their inheritance to the next generation. In this new form of governance, which will build on the successful shoulders of the twenty-first century democracies, every citizen would start their life at the age of twenty-one years, with no wealth inherited from their parents or any relatives/ friends. From that point on, each of those citizens are free to amass as much wealth as they can, legally, without any encumbrances, and at the time of their death (or their partners' death), that wealth will be passed on to the state. The state will invest the property and wealth (from the citizens that have passed away) into education, infrastructure projects, defence, law enforcement and social services to take care of the sick and the disabled.

Where did the idea originate?

This idea came about as a thought experiment in discussions between the author and some of his close friends. It was clear to them, looking at the societies across the globe, that the current structure of capitalistic democracies is untenable. These capitalistic democracies function well for a single generation but their core design breaks down when applied across multiple generations. Over a period of time (say over hundred years), the rich get richer and the poor get poorer, leading to an ever-widening wealth and income gap. In the past, these widening gaps were reset by bloody revolutions including the French revolution in the 18th century and the Bolshevik revolution in the 19th century serving as strong examples.

This issue, of ever widening gap between haves and have nots as well as the lack of a level playing field for each new generation, has occupied the author's mind for the longest time. And having researched the genesis of democracy around 500 BC (with Cleisthenes letting go of some of his absolute power to establish senate to stabilize government in Athens), establishment of 'magna carta' in 12th century England, and 'bill of rights' in 18th century USA, it became clear that each of those step changes were instrumental in getting humanity to its current state of freedom and minimal tyranny from the prevailing government.

In order for India and the current generation to make life better for the future generations, we need to look at "inheritance" as the other side of the coin of "bonded labour". We abolished bond labour (where kids of bonded labour would in turn become bonded labour until released by their masters) at the start of the 20th century. That was a very good collective decision by all progressive societies. We need to make a similar call on abolishing "inheritance". Just to be clear, all progressive societies should require every citizen, once they turn 21 yrs of age, to start their life with a clean slate. Nobody receives any inheritance, and everyone will have to make their living on their own. This way the playing field is level for all and everyone has the opportunity to reach full potential regardless of who they were born to. Granted this will not address all inequalities such as genetic disparities, access to better social networks while growing up, etc., but it will still address the key disparity that can be addressed through changing policy.

Pokhran is a fictional story to package that idea in a fiction format. Also, the book is a tribute to the author's origins as well as to a close friend of the author, who was born with significant disabilities. *Pokhran*, by design, doesn't lay out the idea (of a society without inheritance) as an explicit in our face proposal. Instead, it is presented as a subtle idea to be discovered by the readers. The hope here is that one of the readers of this book (with political aspirations) might read this and regard it as her/his "find" and pursue the establishment of such a society in their proposed administration.

Is this another form of communism?

No. In Paracratic society, every individual will have the freedom for free enterprise and can accumulate as much wealth as they like in their lifetime. The only thing that they (and everybody else) won't be able to do is to pass on that wealth to their next generation. As opposed to communism, where nobody could engage in free enterprise and everyone had to be restricted not to get ahead of anybody else (hence public sector enterprises, upper ceilings on pay for the citizens, etc.,)

Why is levelling the playing field important?

If you imagine life to be a race, it is important that everyone starts at the same level of starting blocks, otherwise the game will be skewed right from the get go.

How does it impact or benefit those that might otherwise have benefited from receiving such an inheritance?

Despite initial surface level reservations around such a society stifling human enterprise and creativity, after deeper thought it becomes evident that such a society will unlock human potential not only for those who come from impoverished backgrounds (they have always been hungry and hence driven/motivated to succeed) but also for those who were brought up in elite households as they will have to start from ground zero once they turn twenty-one. Such a start will ensure that even the children of the super wealthy will be motivated to work hard.

How is it different from estate tax?

Estate tax will reduce the amount of inheritance (e.g., 40% of one million of currency is still 400K), but not necessarily level the playing field for all.

Does this levelling the playing field hold true for other aspects like genetics, social networks, access to information and pedigree?

It does not address the fact that genetics, social networks, access to information and pedigree won't be made equal with change in the way societies will be organized. Even though it may feel like a lot will still remain unaddressed, addressing the generational wealth gap will be a big step forward for all of humanity. As humanity continues to make technological progress, it will be up to the future generations to investigate the potential to level playing field on other aspects such as genetics, social networks, etc.

Why can't those who believe in such a model unilaterally stop inheritance, rather than make it a universal requirement?

This would leave those individuals (whose parents decide not to bequeath their property and estate to their children) at a disadvantage to the rest of the population (whose parents are likely to pass on their estate and wealth to the next generation). Hence it is an all or none approach to setting up the rules of the society, and the required change can't be driven in an incremental or unilateral fashion.